Effective Addiction Treatment:

The Minnesota Alternative

First Edition - Revised January 2013

Paula DeSanto
MS, LSW, CPRP, CCDP-D

Authors copyright ©2012 by PaulaDeSanto

Minnesota Alternatives, LLC
7766 NE Hwy. 65
Spring Lake Park, MN 55432
763-789-4895
www.mnalternatives.com

Title ID: 3951537
ISBN-13: 978-1478332435

Cover design and photography by Rene Trujillo at www.OptoSplash.com

Final editing by Mindy Beller

About the Author:

Paula DeSanto MS, LSW, CPRP, CCDP-D

> Master of Science, Licensed Social Worker, Certified Psychiatric Rehabilitation Practitioner, Certified Co-Occurring Disorders Professional – Diplomate

Paula was trained at the Center for Psychiatric Rehabilitation at Boston University under the leadership of William Anthony, a pioneer of person-centered care for people with psychiatric disorders. She then received training from Dr. Kenneth Minkoff and Dr. David Mee-Lee in person-centered/stage-specific treatment for people with co-occurring disorders. She has a master's degree from Boston University in Psychiatric Rehabilitation Counseling.

Paula has developed programs that serve adults with mental illness and/or addiction issues for over 25 years. She has worked in a variety of settings that include case management, community support, intensive residential and outpatient treatment, and for the Minnesota Department of Human Services Anoka Metro Regional Treatment Center. She is currently the owner and director of Minnesota Alternatives LLC, a program providing consultation, training, and outpatient addiction treatment.

Paula has provided numerous trainings and workshops on co-occurring treatment, client-centered care, emotion-based interventions, and harm/risk reduction.

Paula serves as community faculty for the University of Minnesota in their newly developed Integrated Behavioral Health graduate program teaching about person-centered interventions and the Minnesota Alternative Model of care. She is also on the advisory board for the University of Minnesota's Center for Excellence, leading the state in the development of Integrated Dual Diagnosis Care and plans to work for the Center as a content expert on stage-specific interventions.

Paula is a member of the Community Advisory Board for Medica Behavioral Health, and serves on the Anoka County Directors Network.

She is serving a second 4-year term on the state mental health advisory council after her second appointment to the council by the Governor of Minnesota.

Introduction

The purpose of this guide is to provide the rationale and framework for a new treatment approach called *Effective Addiction Treatment: The Minnesota Alternative*.

I want to acknowledge that Alcoholics Anonymous (AA)/Narcotics Anonymous (NA) and other 12-Step self-help groups have helped countless people recover and improve their lives. They work for many, many people.

However, there are some people, who for various reasons, have not engaged in the self-help movement of AA and/or who have had unsatisfactory experiences with treatment programs using 12-Step facilitation. Alternative approaches are needed.

Minnesota Alternatives, LLC, founded in 2009, is a licensed outpatient program serving adults with addiction disorders. The program provides person-centered treatment with an emphasis on engagement and best practices. Minnesota Alternatives has been incredibly well received by clients, probation officers, county social workers, hospitals, medical and mental health professionals, assessors, educational institutions, judges, lawyers, and all of Minnesota's major health plans (Medica, HealthPartners, Blue Cross Blue Shield, U Care, Preferred One, and Cigna).

I want to recognize and offer sincere thanks to Dr. Kevin Turnquist for his valuable support and assistance. Dr. Turnquist is a strong advocate for person-centered care, and he has provided me numerous hours of consultation and guidance to assist with the development of **humanistic** and science-based interventions. He has co-presented at conferences, endorsed our approach, and has given it the "physician legitimization" needed in a medically driven system. Many of his opinions and articles are included in this guide and more of his writing can be found at www.kevinturnquist.org.

Humanism is a democratic and ethical life stance, which affirms that human beings have the right and responsibility to give meaning and shape to their own lives. It stands for the building of a more humane society through an ethic based on human and other natural values in the spirit of reason and free inquiry through human capabilities.

Thanks to the many people who work to ensure choice, dignity, and self-determination for those in need.

With appreciation,

Paula DeSanto

century addiction treatment program. I only wish that Minnesota Alternatives had been around when I was seeking help for an alcohol problem. I believe that this program is destined to be not the alternative, but the standard of care in the future.

- Kenneth Anderson
  Founder and CEO, HAMS Harm Reduction for Alcohol

- The ideologically driven disease model is being slowly replaced with a science based model that recognizes addiction isn't always progressive, that people have the power to change their behaviors and that harm reduction is effective.

  Minnesota Alternative's is among those few programs based on current research about how best to help those who want either to reduce their consumption or to abstain. It integrates harm reduction, the utilization of neuroplasticity, motivational techniques, and other proven strategies in its person-centered approach.

  This succinct and very readable book clearly describes the successful Minnesota Alternative approach to 12-Step programs. It is well-organized, well-written, and includes extensive Appendices. It is highly recommended, especially to those seeking help with an addiction problem.

  - David J. Hanson, Ph.D.
    Professor Emeritus of Sociology of the State University of New York at Potsdam

- Paula DeSanto's *Effective Addiction Treatment: The Minnesota Alternative* really does provide a new alternative to standard treatments. Her book utilizes recent findings in neuroscience as well as ancient traditions like meditation to describe a treatment for addictions that is comprehensive yet person-centered.

  Bravo Ms. DeSanto!

  - Bruce Field, M.D.
    Medical Director, Building Resilient Families, Resource Recovery Center
    Staff Psychiatrist, Center for International Health
    Consulting Psychiatrist, Center for Victims of Torture

Foreword

Paula DeSanto's *Effective Addiction Treatment: The Minnesota Alternative* is the entry into a new era, with Ms. DeSanto as the guide.

This new era recognizes that a lot of people are not being served by the current standard model for addiction treatment, known as the Minnesota Model, and generally meaning 12-Step therapy and AA. It is ironic—but indicative—that Ms. DeSanto has developed her alternative approach, and flourished, in the "belly of the beast," so to speak. Because even (or should that be "especially") in Minnesota, mental health specialists recognize the need for additional treatment equipment for helping the host of people who currently fall between the cracks. These include many people with simultaneous mental health and addiction issues, people who react poorly to AA and the 12-Step approach, and others who are simply not prepared—or able—to achieve abstinence, either immediately, or even perhaps in the long run. Indeed, for many with mental health conditions, complete abstinence from all medications affecting mood and mind can hardly be immediately and completely withdrawn. The alternative is "harm reduction," or life improvement in the absence of total abstinence.

But let's start at the beginning. Ms. De Santo has worked for a long time in the Minnesota mental health system, where her low-key, humanistic, client-centered approach has attracted clients and fellow mental health specialists alike. Ms. DeSanto obviously wants to help people, obviously does help them, and at the same time doesn't take herself overly seriously. So, what's not to like?

Along with her humanity and her awareness of the need for alternatives, Ms. DeSanto brings an inspiring manner, fortified by her familiarity with—her use of—the entire range of evidence-based helping techniques, as filtered through her own long personal experience as a helper. She presents these methods in an easy-to-comprehend and practical format in "The Minnesota Alternative."

But Ms. DeSanto is doing more than providing a step-by-step manual (although she is doing that as well). She is ushering in a new way of thinking. In the first place, she embodies the new comprehension of recovery that mental health and addiction specialists are coming to, as represented by the Substance Abuse and Mental Health Services Administration's (SAMHSA) recent redefinition of "recovery" as "a process of change through which individuals improve their health and wellness, live a self-directed life and strive to reach their full potential." This opposes focusing solely—or primarily—on abstinence.

SAMHSA is merely catching up to where Ms. DeSanto has been for the last decade or so and to the outpatient clinic she runs that applies this approach to recovery for people with a broad range of mental health and substance issues. This is no theoretical paradigm; it is a living, breathing philosophy that Ms. DeSanto applies skillfully—on a daily basis.

Another sign of the modernity, but also the long-term relevance, of Ms. DeSanto's work is the attention it pays to neuroscience. Except, in a brilliant about-face, Ms. DeSanto doesn't use neuroscience to convince people that their brains have been hijacked. Instead, she helps them to see that—through meditation and other mindfulness techniques—they can take charge of their brain's chemistry to bring their neuro-functioning into line with their goals and desires. Once again, per the new SAMSHA definition of recovery, Ms. DeSanto is assisting people to determine and direct their lives, rather than fostering hopelessness and defeatism.

So please take a long look at, think about, and make use of *Effective Addiction Treatment: The Minnesota Alternative.*

It will not only help you, your clients, and others you care for and about. It will speed along the needed emergence of a whole new helping paradigm in the addiction and mental health fields, one that is long overdue.

Stanton Peele, Ph.D.
Founder of the Life Process Program for addiction treatment

Table of Contents

Effective Addition Treatment:
The Minnesota Alternative

Chapter One

Paradigm Change

Background Information

Paradigm change is underway. Many factors are contributing to the development of new approaches for addiction treatment. These include leaders in the field teaching about person-centered care, scientific advances, evidence-based practices, research on substance use patterns, new definitions of both addiction and recovery, and consumer desire for alternative approaches.

This chapter describes many factors leading to paradigm change, and outlines the primary reasons for the development of a new model: The Minnesota Alternative.

Scientific Advances

We can now study the functional brain. Advances in neuroscience have great implications for the delivery of addiction treatments that allow for brain "opportunities" instead of brain "illness".

The brain is very powerful because it is so sensitive to experience. Where we place our attention defines us at a neurological level and we have far more power to alter our brains, our behaviors, and our personalities than previously thought possible. There are many ways to train our brains. Some techniques include: focused concentration, mindfulness, repetition, mental rehearsal, positive experiences/emotions, and new and novel experiences.[1] These methods can help us to change our thoughts, our emotions, and our behaviors.

Practitioners often describe addiction as "hijacking" the brain, implying that if one struggles with addiction, the brain is out of his or her control. The problem with this theory is that it fails to take into consideration that many people recover from addictive behaviors on their own.[2] It also fails to recognize that the command center of the brain, the

---

[1] Dispenza, J. (2007) *Evolve Your Brain: The Science of Changing Your Mind.*

[2] National Institute of Alcoholism and Alcohol Abuse (2006), *National Epidemiologic Survey on Alcohol and Related Conditions* (NESARC) #70.

frontal lobe, when engaged, can quiet the midbrain. In fact, mindfulness practices have been shown to quiet the different regions of the brain that make up the "craving network".[3]

Clients have displayed strong enthusiasm and interest in learning about how their brains work. They feel empowered knowing they can learn to engage their frontal lobes, thus improving their ability to self-regulate. A client commented, "I have been in so many treatment programs and the only tools I leave with are to go to AA (Alcoholics Anonymous) meetings and get a sponsor. Now I have a bunch of tools. I have learned how to use my brain to think greater than how I feel, and I have learned many skills to help me think differently."

Policy Recommendations and Evidenced-Based Practices

System change can be very difficult, and is often met with resistance. However, national organizations are promoting change by defining policy and practice recommendations based on research-informed and evidence-based practices. They are also increasing public access to research information. Providers are increasingly held accountable to produce measureable outcomes.

The National Institute on Alcohol Abuse and Alcoholism (NIAAA), the National Institute on Drug Abuse (NIDA), and the Substance Abuse and Mental Health Services Administration (SAMHSA) have come forth with policy recommendations that emphasize the need for person-centered interventions. To highlight a few:[4]

- No single treatment is appropriate for everyone. Matching treatment settings, interventions, and services to an individual's particular problems and needs is critical to his or her ultimate success in returning to productive functioning in the family, workplace, and society.

- Research shows that combining treatment medications, where available, with behavioral therapy is the best way to ensure success for most patients. Treatment approaches must be tailored to address each patient's drug-abuse patterns and drug-related medical, psychiatric, and social problems.

- Addiction can affect so many aspects of a person's life, and treatment must address the needs of the whole person to be successful. This is why the best programs incorporate a variety of rehabilitative services into their comprehensive treatment regimens.

- NIDA recommends that treatment programs include:

---

[3] McGonigal, K. (2011) *How Mindfulness Makes the Brain Immune to Temptation*. The Science of Willpower.

[4] National Institute of Drug Abuse (2009) *Principles of Effective Treatment: A Research-Based Guide* (2nd edition).

- ° Cognitive Behavioral Therapy
- ° Motivational Incentives
- ° Motivational Interviewing
- ° Group Therapy
- ° A menu of services that includes medical, psychological, social, vocational, and legal support.

Research on Substance Use Patterns

Another factor contributing to paradigm change is research on patterns of drug and alcohol use. Addiction is often referenced as chronic and progressive. While this may be the case for some, it is not true for most. Research shows that the majority of people who meet the criteria for substance dependence do not continue to meet the criteria over time.

In 2001/2002, NIAAA conducted the National Epidemiologic Survey on Alcohol and Related Conditions (NESARC), the largest study ever conducted (sample size of n = 43,093) and concluded:[5]

- Twenty years after the onset of alcohol dependence, about three-fourths of individuals are in full recovery; more than half of those who have fully recovered drink at low-risk levels without symptoms of alcohol dependence.

- Many heavy drinkers do not have alcohol dependence. For example, even in people who have five or more drinks a day (the equivalent of a bottle of wine) the rate of developing dependence is less than 7 percent per year.

According to a publication from NIDA, *Drugs, Brains, and Behavior: The Science of Addiction*, drug abuse starts early, peaks in teen years, and rarely occurs in older adults.[6] Age is a limiting factor in the use of drugs and alcohol. One longitudinal study showed no initiation into alcohol or cigarette use after age 29, and very little first-time use of any other drugs after that age. In fact, most people stopped using illicit drugs by age 29. Daily users of alcohol and marijuana decreased their use by this age and only cigarette smokers continued to use and increase daily use with age.[7]

The Disease Discussion

Jellinek (1960), in his study of alcoholism, put forth the notion of alcoholism as a disease. He drew his study sample from members of AA.[8] In modern day usage, the disease model asserts that addiction is a primary disease, has no cure, often involves denial and loss of

---

[5] National Institute of Alcoholism and Alcohol Abuse (2006) *National Epidemiologic Survey on Alcohol and Related Conditions* (NESARC) #70.

[6] National Institute of Drug Abuse (2009) *Drugs, Brains, and Behavior: The Science of Addiction.*

[7] Chen, K., & Kandel, D. (1995) The natural history of drug use from adolescence to the mid-thirties in a general population sample. *American Journal of Public Health*, 85, 41-47.

[8] Jellinekk, E. (1960) *The disease concept of alcoholism.* New Haven, CT: Hilllhouse.

control, and inevitably progresses toward disaster if the disease process is not arrested. Recovery is a lifelong process of containment that can be achieved only by abstinence from all psychoactive substances.[9]

The question of whether or not a substance use disorder is a disease is a hot topic and has stimulated discussions on blogs, on-line discussion groups and scientific commentary.

Some conclude that drug and alcohol use is a disease because it can disturb a person's normal hierarchy of needs and desires and disrupt brain circuits involved in memory and behavioral control.

Others question this thinking. According to Dr. Kevin Turnquist, "Drugs and alcohol have an impact on the brain and the body, but so do lots of other factors such as stress, strong emotions, loneliness, or trauma. The "disease" argument could be applied to any number of environmental variables that result in brain changes that are not welcome or positive. By that standard, loneliness is also a disease. It results in chemical and even structural brain changes that predispose people to anxiety, depression, and insomnia".

Over the course of history, many models have been used to describe addictions. These include:

- Moral Model: Freely chosen "immoral" behavior, a lack of discipline, or a lack of willpower. Calls for punishment.
- Medical Model: Chronic and progressive disease. Genetic factors increase risk.
- Spiritual Model: Pride versus humility and resentment versus acceptance. Use to fill a spiritual emptiness and restore health through a higher power.
- Psychological Model: Deficits in learning, emotional/mental health, or behavioral causes.
- Social Cultural Model: Emphasis on socioeconomic status, cultural and ethnic beliefs, family norms.

SAMHSA has concluded that research confirms some truth in each model. The field has now recognized the importance of many interacting influences and now endorses a composite biopsychosocial-spiritual model.[10]

Dr. Gabor Maté, in his book, *In the Realm of Hungry Ghosts*, defines addiction in simple terms: "Addiction is any repeated behavior, substance-related or not, in which a person feels compelled to persist, regardless of its negative impact on his or her life and the lives of others".

---

[9] Denning, P., Little, J. (2012) *Practicing Harm Reduction Psychotherapy,* 2nd Edition.

[10] SAMHSA Treatment Improvement Protocol, #35 *Enhancing Motivation for Change in Substance Abuse Treatment.*

At the time of this writing, the DSM IV (R) is under revision and the DSM V is due to be released in May 2013. Presently there is a great deal of discussion and controversy about the proposed changes. Upon review, there may be a risk of many more people becoming diagnosed with addiction disorders, but the changes may also help reduce the "one size fits all" mindset that is so prevalent in the current system.

According to the American Psychiatric Association (APA):[11]

"Among the Substance-Related Disorders Work Group proposals is the recommendation that the diagnostic category include both substance use disorders and non-substance addictions. Gambling disorder has been moved into this category and there are other addiction-like behavioral disorders such as 'Internet Addiction' that will be considered as potential additions to this category as research data accumulates."

"Further, the work group has proposed to tentatively re-title the category, 'Addiction and Related Disorders'. The work group had extensive discussions on the use of the word "addiction." There was general agreement that "dependence" as a label for compulsive, out-of-control drug use has been problematic. It has been confusing to physicians and has resulted in patients with normal tolerance and withdrawal being labeled as "addicts." This has also resulted in patients suffering from severe pain having adequate doses of opioids withheld due to fear of producing "addiction." Accordingly, the word 'dependence' is now limited to physiological dependence, which is a normal response to repeated doses of many medications including beta-blockers, antidepressants, opioids, anti-anxiety agents and other drugs. The presence of tolerance and withdrawal symptoms are not counted as symptoms of substance use disorder when occurring in the context of appropriate medical treatment with prescribed medications."

These recommendations also include identifying the severity of the disorder as mild, moderate, or severe. They also acknowledge that many appropriately prescribed medications produce physiological dependence. The proposed changes also address the serious problem of "addicts" not having access to needed pain management medications.

In general, Minnesota Alternatives discourages identification with "labels" and instead focuses on person-centered language: We are people who abuse substances or experience addiction, or people who suffer from depression or schizophrenia. We are people first, not "addicts" or "schizophrenics".

_____

[11] American Psychiatric Association (APA) *Diagnostic and Statistical Manual of Mental Disorders, 4th Edition*, Text Revision. Washington, DC: APA, 2000.

My professional experience reinforces the need for individualized responses. Some people have clearly progressed to the point of having a chronic and progressive disease, while others experience serious use but are then able to moderate and return to non-problematic use. For the latter group, education and supportive counseling are often enough to reestablish non-problematic substance use patterns.

This point is illustrated in the following examples.

Consider a 45-year-old nurse, who has lost her job and has also been divorced by her husband. She starts to drink more to cope with depression and loneliness. She has difficulty sleeping and is prescribed sleeping pills and benzodiazepines to help with her anxiety. She begins taking more than she is prescribed to help numb out and sleep her days away. Before long, she meets the criteria for substance dependence. She then seeks out therapy and learns key coping skills to manage difficult emotions and gets emotional support for her losses. She decides to stop drinking and begins to take her medications as ordered. She finds a new job and enters into a healthy relationship. She effectively uses her coping skills and becomes skilled at mindfulness and emotion regulation. She returns to social drinking and continues to take medications when needed for sleep and anxiety.

By contrast, a 65-year-old man has been drinking whiskey for over 30 years, leading to multiple health issues secondary to alcohol use. If he doesn't drink every day he experiences symptoms of withdrawal. He has tried to quit several times by self-admitting himself for detoxification and treatment, but never manages to stay sober longer than a few days. He has lost his family and friends over the years and now spends most of his time drinking. His use is chronic and progressive, and abstinence seems essential to maintaining a reasonable quality of life.

Defining Recovery

Is the nurse (who still drinks) described above in recovery? She is, according to SAMHSA's newly revised (2011) definition of recovery.[12] "In recovery" used to mean someone who is abstinent after a struggle with substance use. The definition no longer includes the need for abstinence and emphasizes the unique paths each person takes toward recovery.

SAMHSA's definition in 2009: "Recovery from alcohol and drug problems is a process of change through which an individual achieves abstinence and improved health, wellness, and quality of life."

---

[12] SAMHSA Press Release (2011) *SAMHSA announces a working definition of "recovery" from mental disorders and substance use disorders.*

SAMHSA's definition is 2011: "Recovery from Mental Disorders and Substance Use Disorders: A process of change through which individuals improve their health and wellness, live a self-directed life, and strive to reach their full potential."

Through the Recovery Support Strategic Initiative, SAMHSA has also delineated four major dimensions that support a life in recovery:

- *Health* : overcoming or managing one's disease(s) as well as living in a physically and emotionally healthy way
- *Home*: a stable and safe place to live
- *Purpose*: meaningful daily activities, such as a job, school, volunteerism, family caretaking, or creative endeavors, and the independence, income, and resources to participate in society
- *Community*: relationships and social networks that provide support, friendship, love, and hope

SAMHSA has identified the following guiding principles of recovery:

Recovery emerges from hope: The belief that recovery is real provides the essential and motivating message of a better future: that people can and do overcome the internal and external challenges, barriers, and obstacles that confront them.

Recovery is person-driven: Self-determination and self-direction are the foundations for recovery as individuals define their own life goals and design their unique paths.

Recovery occurs via many pathways: Individuals are unique with distinct needs, strengths, preferences, goals, cultures, and backgrounds, including trauma experiences that affect and determine their pathways to recovery. Abstinence is the safest approach for those with substance use disorders.

Recovery is holistic: Recovery encompasses an individual's whole life, including mind, body, spirit, and community. The array of services and supports available should be integrated and coordinated.

Recovery is supported by peers and allies: Mutual support and mutual aid groups that include the sharing of experiential knowledge and skills, as well as social learning, play an invaluable role in recovery.

Recovery is supported through relationship and social networks: An important factor in the recovery process is the presence and involvement of people who believe in the person's ability to recover; who offer hope, support, and encouragement; and who also suggest strategies and resources for change.

Recovery is culturally-based and influenced: Culture and cultural background in all of its diverse representations (including values, traditions, and beliefs) are keys in determining a person's journey and unique pathway to recovery.

Recovery is supported by addressing trauma: Services and supports should be trauma-informed to foster safety (physical and emotional) and trust, as well as promote choice, empowerment, and collaboration.

Recovery involves individual, family, community strengths, and responsibility: Individuals, families, and communities have strengths and resources that serve as a foundation for recovery.

Recovery is based on respect: Community, systems, societal acceptance, and appreciation for people affected by mental health and substance use problems – including protecting their rights and eliminating discrimination – are crucial in achieving recovery.

The above sections identify numerous factors contributing to paradigm change, but the primary motive for starting Minnesota Alternatives and writing this practice guide is hearing story after story of high levels of dissatisfaction with previous treatment experiences.

Consumer Desire for Alternatives

More than 90% of alcohol and drug treatment programs in the U.S. are based on the 12 steps of AA (SAMSHA, 2010)[13]. Providers incorporate AA, yet often do not practice AA's inclusive principles.

A colleague shares his perspective:

"Treatment providers can learn from the way AA accepts people who may be ambivalent about abstinence, rather than require people to commit to abstinence as a condition for treatment. AA accepts people into a meeting even if they arrive with alcohol on their breath, while treatment providers often send people away or may even discharge them. AA says "progress not perfection". Treatment providers say commit to abstinence even if you aren't ready for that and then be perfect or we discharge you – and by the way, we are an honest program so don't lie about using, but we'll kick you out if you are honest and tell me you use; or we'll try to catch you with random drug screens."

---

[13] SAMHSA Press Release (2010) Office of Applied Studies. _The N-SSATS report. Clinical or therapeutic approaches used by substance abuse treatment facilities._ Rockville, MD: US Dept. of Health and Human Services.

Almost 30 years of clinical experience and working in a variety of settings have provided me a rich opportunity to serve clients throughout the continuum of care. During this time, many clients have expressed how treatment has been ineffective and unsatisfying. Multiple clients have gone so far as to describe their experiences as torture.

Frequent client comments include:

- "I was just a number to them, nobody really cared."
- "All they do is herd people in and out to make money."
- "The groups were so big, nobody shared anything real."
- "The staff just talks at you, not with you."
- "It was just a game – people said one thing in group but then went out to smoke and talked about their plans to get high."
- "All you do is complete steps 1 through 3 over and over, fill out the papers, when and how they want you to, and then you are considered successfully treated."
- "I don't believe in the steps but I did them just to graduate."
- "It was not safe to talk about what was really going on because then they would kick you out."
- "I don't identify with being powerless. I am not powerless."
- "I don't like the concept of surrendering to a higher power."
- "A great deal of time is focused on negative things instead of hope or positive thoughts."
- "I was not given any tools for recovery other than go to meetings and find a sponsor."

During an interview with a woman, she shared that she had been kicked out of a residential treatment program because she was "toxic" to the therapeutic setting. She went on to explain that she was asked to leave for questioning the principle of surrender, as she did not find this concept helpful. These negative experiences are disheartening, along with the message clients receive about being toxic or a failure.

Failure was a frequent occurrence, but perhaps it was the treatment that was failing the person, not the person failing the treatment.

Chapter Two

Person-Centered Interventions

Addiction can affect so many aspects of a person's life, and treatment must address the needs of the whole person to be successful.

The diversity of substance users calls for inclusive, flexible, and comprehensive models. Initiatives supporting paradigm change challenge providers to focus on the needs of each individual instead of using a "one size fits all" approach. This chapter outlines examples of person-centered approaches, identifies barriers to system change, and concludes with information about harm reduction.

A client shares his experience:

"When I first started at Minnesota Alternatives, I managed to stay sober 7 weeks. I ended up relapsing and continued to do so. I tried to control my use for 14 months but wasn't able to reach my harm reduction goals. Then, one day, during a group check-in, I became flooded with emotion. I haven't used since that day 9 ½ months ago."

"Minnesota Alternatives has helped me get on a path where I don't engage in self-destructive behavior. I continually learn to deal with my negative thoughts and emotions in a constructive way. The program's emphasis on relaxed breathing and meditation were especially helpful to me."

"The harm reduction approach worked for me because using was always an option. External pressure to quit was not as effective as letting the internal pressure build and culminate in an emotional release. The staff was skilled at letting me discover for myself the benefit of a healthy lifestyle instead of telling me how things 'should' be."

Motivational Interviewing and the Stage of Change Model have gained a lot of attention and many states are encouraging providers to adopt these practices. Motivational Interviewing is a method that works on facilitating and engaging intrinsic motivation within the client in order to change behavior. The Stage of Change Model identifies the different steps most people go through during the process of change.

Stage of Change Model (SCM)

The Stages of Change Model was originally developed in the late 1970s and early 1980s by James Prochaska and Carlo DiClemente, at the University of Rhode Island while they were studying how smokers were able to give up their habits or addictions.[14] It recognizes that behavior change does not happen in one step, and people tend to progress through different stages on their way to successful change.

Expecting behavior change by simply telling someone who is still in the "pre-contemplation" stage that he or she must go to a certain number of AA meetings in a certain time period is perhaps counterproductive, because by definition, the individual at this stage is not ready to change. For example, many people are mandated by the court to attend treatment and they may not think they need intervention.

Each person must decide when a stage is completed and when to move on to the next stage. This decision must come from the inside. Stable, long-term change cannot be externally imposed. Interventions match the person's stage of change.

The Stages of Change:	Interventions:
Pre-Contemplation: I do not have a problem with drugs or alcohol. My problems are caused by other people who tend to make my life more difficult.	Make empathy the priority. Provide practical assistance, outreach if possible, and focus on engagement. Create a welcoming atmosphere and work on anything the client is open to addressing. Provide incentives for engagement.
Contemplation: I may or may not have a problem. It is possible that my use of drugs or alcohol is causing problems in my life, but I am not certain.	Explore ambivalence and the pros and cons of substance use. Do not take sides. Provide encouragement and instill hope. Provide education and continued emphasis on engagement. Continue with practical assistance.
Preparation: Change talk emerges. I agree that I have a problem and I am ready to start planning for change.	Encourage commitment to change. Try things out, make agreements. Provide education and skills training and practical tools that generalize easily to the client's life.
Action: I am certain that my use of drugs or alcohol is causing problems and I am ready to do something about it, or I have already started to make changes.	Help establish steps that foster success. Set up plans for high risk-situations. Reinforce changes. Continue education and skill development.
Maintenance: I have been taking steps, and I no longer use drugs or alcohol, or they are no longer causing problems in my life.	Plan for relapse prevention. Continue to address whole person and other needs.

---

[14] Prochaska, J. O., DiClemente, C. C. (2005) The transtheoretical approach. In: Norcross, JC; Goldfried, MR. (eds.) Handbook of psychotherapy integration. 2nd ed. New York: Oxford University Press.

Motivational Interviewing

Motivational Interviewing is a semi-directive, client-centered counseling style for eliciting behavior change by helping clients explore and resolve ambivalence.[15] Compared with non-directive counseling, it is more focused and goal-directed. Motivational Interviewing is a method that works on facilitating and engaging intrinsic motivation in order to change behavior. The examination and resolution of ambivalence is a central purpose, and the counselor is intentionally directive in pursuing this goal.

Motivational Interviewing recognizes and accepts that clients approach counseling at different levels of readiness for change.

Motivational interviewing includes four basic skills:

- O – The ability to ask open-ended questions
- A – The ability to provide affirmations
- R – The capacity for reflective listening
- S – The ability to periodically provide summary statements to the client

Motivational Interviewing departs from traditional client-centered therapy through the use of direction, in which therapists attempt to influence clients to consider making changes.

Motivational Interviewing is based upon four general principles:

- **Express Empathy** – This involves trying to fully understand the client's perspective, meaning clients are validated and heard. This promotes engagement, trust, disclosure, and a sense of belonging.

- **Support Self-Efficacy** – Client's belief and hope that change is possible is essential for change. Clients are held responsible for choosing and carrying out actions and there is no "right way" to change.

- **Roll with Resistance** – The counselor does not fight client resistance, but "rolls with it." Resistance is not challenged and instead the counselor uses the client's "momentum" to further explore the client's views. Motivational Interviewing encourages clients to develop their own solutions to their identified problems. Thus, there is no real hierarchy in the client-counselor relationship for the client to fight against.

- **Develop Discrepancy** – Motivation for change occurs when people perceive a discrepancy between where they are and where they want to be. Motivational

---

[15] Miller, W. R., Zweben, A., DiClemente, C. C., & Rychtarik, R. G. (1992) *Motivational Enhancement Therapy Manual.*

Interviewing counselors work to develop this through helping clients examine the discrepancies between their current behavior and future goals.

Barriers to System Change

Despite the focus on person-centered approaches by both national and state leadership, many providers are reluctant to integrate these methods. There are many reasons why providers are slow to change and some of the possible barriers are outlined below:

Barrier:	Ways to Address Barrier:
Very large systems of care are based on 12-Step methods. AA/Narcotics Anonymous (NA) offer broad community support.	Alternatives are starting to emerge, and will become more common as demand for new approaches continues to grow.
Many providers have used the 12 Steps as the path to their own recovery and feel strongly that this is the only way.	AA works for many people, but not for others. Focus on what works. Educational institutions are producing a work force that is trained in person-centered approaches, and as staff turnover occurs, the newly trained workforce will introduce different treatment interventions.
Service delivery is set up as episodes of treatment and does not provide continuity of care, long-term support.	Services need to be restructured to allow for long-term support with seamless access for more intensive services when needed. This requires a greater emphasis on outreach and care coordination instead of treatment.
Group intervention is primary (often large groups) and many programs don't provide individual counseling.	Programs and systems of care may need to restructure and find ways to increase client/staff ratios. Each client should have individualized attention and a treatment plan that reflects his or her unique goals.
Harm reduction is perceived by some as an "excuse to let people use".	Harm reduction is a set of principles to help guide program development and interventions, and it includes the full range of harm-reducing goals including abstinence.
Organizational change is difficult.	Change can happen in small incremental steps and does not require a complete program overhaul.

Despite multiple barriers, change is happening. Clients are asserting their desire for alternative approaches, health plans are eager to purchase new models of care, legislative bodies are mandating best practices and certifications/credentialing for clinicians, and academic institutions are training a workforce in person-centered interventions.

Working with people at all stages of change prioritizes engagement, and allows for early intervention before more serious consequences occur. Effective treatment for someone who does not think he or she has a problem, or does not endorse abstinence as a goal, requires programs to incorporate principles of harm reduction.

Understanding Harm Reduction

Harm Reduction is a concept that is frequently misunderstood. While presenting at a conference, an addiction psychiatrist was asked about his views on harm reduction. He stated he did not support it, but then went on to share numerous client scenarios that included harm reduction strategies; however, he referenced them as "risk reduction".

At a different conference, another addiction psychiatrist was asked about his views on harm reduction. He replied, "Are you kidding? That is all I do! I try to find ways to help people feel better or improve the quality of their life. Everybody makes choices that have negative impacts on their health, and I try to reduce the harm of those choices."

Stage-wise treatment is a person-centered, humanistic approach, and is also considered a best practice. To provide it inherently means providing treatment for people who may not want to quit using, and many substance users avoid seeking help because they do not have a goal of life-long abstinence. Accepting goals other than abstinence opens the door to this group of people.

Harm reduction does not equate to continued use. Harm-reduction approaches embrace the full range of harm-reducing goals including abstinence. Abstinence, as a harm-reduction strategy, is chosen by many.

At a meeting of addiction professionals, someone challenged our approach and stated that supporting anything other than a goal of abstinence for someone who meets the criteria for substance dependence is unethical. My response, "Imposing goals on people and not meeting them where they are seems unethical."

What is Harm Reduction?[16]

Harm reduction first emerged as a public health alternative to the moral/criminal and disease models of drug use and addiction. Originally geared toward active substance users

---

[16] Harm Reduction Coalition. *Principles of Harm Reduction.*

who were unable or unwilling to stop using, harm reduction became accepted in the United States in the late 1980s and early 1990s as a set of public health strategies for reducing the spread of human immunodeficiency virus (HIV) and other risks associated with active substance use.

The essence is the pragmatic recognition that treatment must meet active substance users "where they are" in terms of their needs and personal goals. Thus, harm reduction approaches embrace the full range of harm-reducing goals including, but not limited to, abstinence. This means small incremental positive changes are seen as steps in the right direction. Positive steps enhance self-efficacy and hope, which in turn make change possible.

Principles of Harm Reduction

- Substances have multiple meanings and adaptive values to people. These include self-medication, coping with negative emotions, sense of identity, personality integrator, liberator of creativity, and a primary source of pleasure. Given the function that substances play in people's lives, users often have a desire to moderate, or reduce the harm, without stopping altogether.

- Cessation of drug use does not have to be the first goal of intervention or the sole measure of successful treatment. Service providers meet clients where they are, not where they would like them to be, and establish quality of individual and community life and well-being – not necessarily cessation of drug use – as the criteria for successful interventions and policies.

- Many clients have not made a decision to stop or may state they wish to continue to use, but still need assistance. Non-judgmental, non-coercive service providers can be effective helpers with clients anywhere along the continuum of drug use.

- Harm reduction acknowledges that licit and illicit drug use is part of our world and works to minimize its harmful effects rather than simply ignore or condemn them; and it recognizes that the realities of poverty, class, racism, social isolation, past trauma, and other social inequalities affect people's vulnerability to and capacity for effectively dealing with drug-related harms.

- Harm reductions understands drug use as a complex, multi-faceted phenomenon that encompasses a continuum of behaviors from severe abuse to total abstinence, and acknowledges that some ways of using drugs are clearly safer than others.

- It ensures that drug users and those with a history of drug use routinely have a real voice in the creation of programs and policies designed to serve them and affirms drug users themselves as the primary agents of reducing the harms of their drug use (Harm Reduction Coalition).

Examples of harm reduction strategies to reduce use or reduce the consequences of use include:

- Syringe exchange
- Methadone, Suboxone
- Benzodiazepines
- Cannabis
- Designated driver
- Ignition interlock

Is Harm Reduction an Evidenced-Based Practice?

In his report on harm reduction evidence, Neil Hunt (2010) reviews hundreds of studies on the efficacy of harm-reduction interventions. The report summarizes practices that have shown efficacy in reducing drug-related harm under eight categories including: needle and other syringe programs; methadone and other replacement therapies; heroin prescribing; de-penalization; information, education, and communication; safe injecting and other drug consumption rooms; pill testing and allied warning systems; and motivational interviewing.[17]

The low prevalence (approximately 1%) of HIV among injecting drug users reflects the early adoption and rapid expansion of harm reduction in Australia. Countries that have provided extensive needle and syringe programs and opioid substitution treatment appear to have averted an epidemic, stabilized, or substantially reduced the prevalence of HIV among injecting drug users. However, despite decades of vigorous advocacy and scientific evidence, the global coverage of needle and syringe programs and opioid substitution treatment falls well short of the levels required to achieve international HIV control (NSW Public Health Bulletin, 2010).[18]

A report titled the *Global Commission on Drug Policy Report*[19] has gained a lot of attention. The 19-person commission composed of prominent leaders from across the globe as well as representatives from the US, challenges the conventional wisdom about drug markets and drug use: "The global war on drugs has failed, with devastating consequences for individuals and societies around the world. The emphasis in drug policy on harsh law enforcement over four decades has not accomplished its goal of banishing drugs, and has in fact, spawned wide, dramatic eruptions of violence".

---

[17] Hunt, N. (2010). A review of the evidence-base for harm reduction approaches to drug use. *Available at www.ihra.net*
[18] New South Wales Public Health Bulletin. (2010) Mar-Apr;21(3-4):69-73. *Is Harm Reduction Effective?*
[19] *Global Commission on Drug* Policy Report (2011) *The war on drugs and HIV/AIDS: How the criminalization of drug use fuels the global pandemic.*

The report addresses the benefits of approaches designed to reduce harm. The international commission brings an informed, science-based discussion, about humane and effective ways to reduce the harm caused by drugs to people and societies. The report builds on the successful experience of the Latin American Commission on Drugs and Democracy.

The evidence to support harm reduction is clear, but what may be missing are controlled studies to meet the threshold of being scientifically supported. Harm reduction as a whole, based on the development of respectful client-centered therapeutic relationships, adheres to the most important and researched ingredient of successful therapy, the relationship itself.[20]

The Medicinal Use of Addictive Medication/Drugs

Many substance use providers do not permit clients to remain on medications that are addictive. These often include hypnotics, benzodiazepines, stimulants, and opiates. Examples include a young woman who just had knee surgery, but was not allowed to continue in her treatment program due to taking Percocet, even though she had never struggled with opiate use. Another woman started at Minnesota Alternatives because the treatment program she had been attending did not allow her to continue because she was put on Suboxone to help her with a long and painful struggle with heroin.

Emerging efforts to treat addiction point to the potential importance of therapies that provide some low potency, long-term stimulation of the receptors involved in a specific addiction. These *agonist therapies* include current medications such as methadone and buprenorphine (Suboxone) for opioid addiction and varenicline (Chantix) for smoking cessation. Agonist therapies are likely to provide the most effective treatments in the future, as opposed to *antagonist* therapies that block the receptors and thus the effects of the drug. A current example is naltrexone (Vivitrol) for opioid addiction. There is evidence of some effectiveness if external coercion is used, but much less or no effectiveness in other circumstances (Willenbring 2012).

While talking with a couple of psychiatrists, I raised the question about the use of benzodiazepines for treating anxiety in people with substance use disorders. What unfolded was a spirited conversation, with clearly differing ideas and prescribing practices. One felt benzodiazepines should never be used long-term, and that anyone who continued to take them could not be considered "sober". The other was comfortable prescribing them long-term, providing the patient was trustworthy and was not abusing them.

---

[20] Denning, P., Little, J. (2012) *Practicing Harm Reduction Psychotherapy* 2nd Edition (pg. 306).

The following articles, written by Dr. Kevin Turnquist and Dr. Mark Willenbring examine this question.

Klonopin for Patients with Addiction Disorders

First, let's be clear on one thing. No physician – myself included – wants to go on record advocating for the use of Klonopin or other benzodiazepines with people who have addiction disorders.

A review of the literature doesn't provide any articles in support of the practice and warnings abound. No one disputes the fact that all of the drugs in this class can be addictive. They readily produce both tolerance and withdrawal effects. They can impair memory, cause problems with balance, and people shouldn't operate automobiles or other machinery while using them. Some people become disinhibited on them. The common-sense objections to giving people with addictions to alcohol or other drugs of abuse an addicting prescription drug can be almost insurmountable.

Yet there are still occasions in which I'll prescribe Klonopin. How can I explain this?

As a result of humanitarian concerns, some of us clinicians have been engaged in a "Harm Reduction" approach with our patients since before the term came into being. We recognize that there are some people who are simply not going to quickly and consistently embrace abstinence from all mood-altering chemicals. Turning our backs on them, with the message that they should come back for psychiatric treatment only when they're no longer abusing drugs or alcohol, does not seem ethical if we believe that they won't be able to achieve abstinence.

Many of these people suffer from other disorders in addition to their addictions. Anxiety disorders, personality disorders, and sleep disorders are all common in this population. Some clients suffer from schizophrenia or bipolar disorders.

Our clients often have had difficult childhoods. Many have been subjected to various forms of abuse or neglect. An awful lot of them have been through a series of traditional, abstinence-based treatment programs without experiencing any significant periods in which they were free of chemical abuse.

So what we sometimes term "an external locus of control" is frequently found in these clients regardless of their additional diagnoses. This involves a core assumption that relief from one's problems or painful emotional states must come from outside the self. It is a rare human who can accept total responsibility for the problems in his life and count on being able to deal with them on his own.

Ms. DeSanto asked me to comment on the use of benzodiazepines with people who have a chemical dependence, largely because her program sees two of my outpatients and both of them are taking Klonopin.

"Mr. A" is a man who has failed countless chemical dependency treatment programs and had been drinking a 1.5-liter bottle of whiskey per day when I met him. As his history was reviewed, it became apparent to me that in addition to his alcoholism he suffered from both a previously undiagnosed fetal alcohol spectrum disorder and panic disorder. He was quite anxious, impulsive, slept poorly, and had not responded well to any of the many anticonvulsants or antidepressants that had been prescribed over the years. He wasn't interested in any of the other meds that we discussed as potentially helpful but was quite willing to try a low dose of Klonopin.

Benzodiazepines and alcohol are cross-tolerant. If we're trying to detox someone from alcohol, we'll almost always use a benzo to replace the alcohol for a while, then taper off the pills when the alcohol withdrawal is completed. I was trained to detox with Librium. Other docs are more familiar with Valium or Ativan for detoxification. But using benzodiazepines to get people off of alcohol without going through delirium tremens of withdrawal seizures has been the standard of care for many years.

On the unusual occasions that I'll regularly prescribe a minor tranquilizer of the benzodiazepine class for chemical dependency (CD) clients, Klonopin (Clonazepam) is almost always the one I'll choose. Klonopin was originally marketed as an anticonvulsant back in the 1960s, so it may have some mood-stabilizing properties.

In this class, the shorter the action potential of the drug, the greater the subjective "buzz" and the greater potential for abuse. Klonopin has slower on-site action, so it doesn't produce that intense initial effect. The fact that it sticks around in the system so long reduces the chance of withdrawal effects. And I manage my patient's refills myself so if someone is using more Klonopin than I'm prescribing, I'll know about it pretty quickly.

In Mr. A's case, the harm reduction approach has been pretty successful. He hasn't drunk any whiskey at all in several months. He hasn't had a panic attack for about that long either. He never took more Klonopin than prescribed and now a month's prescription will typically last him for 6 weeks or so. He does drink some red wine but he denies ever drinking to intoxication and says that he never uses Klonopin if he's drinking. He attends his program at Minnesota Alternatives regularly, hasn't needed a psychiatric hospitalization, and is now thinking about getting a job. If successful treatment is defined as helping people to have a better life it would be hard to argue that harm reduction hasn't been more useful than any of the other treatment approaches he's gone through.

My other client, "Mr. B", is a young man with bipolar illness that has been hard to manage over the years. He's been through the usual gamut of psychiatric hospitalizations and failed CD treatments too, but he's a bit unusual in that his drugs of choice are cough and cold medicines. Like Mr. A, he had some significant problems that had gone unrecognized in addition to the obvious CD and bipolar issues. It turned out that he had restless leg syndrome, as well as relatively severe daytime anxiety. Adding a small bedtime dose of Klonopin to address the restless legs has helped a great deal with his sleep and he feels calmer during the day. He hasn't shown any tendency to abuse it and he remains active in his chemical dependency program too.

I think that both of these clients would tell you that Klonopin has been very helpful at this time of their lives. They know that I was reluctant to prescribe it for them and that I'd be happier if they didn't take it at all. But the fact that we were willing to spend some time with them and did our best to address all of their problems, seemed to mean a lot to them. Both would readily say that the harm reduction treatment that they've been involved in has been more effective than anything else that they've tried and that their lives are better for it. Ultimately, that's what counts in our business (Turnquist, K., 2010).

Benzodiazepines for Recovering People?

First, I personally think that the idea that no one who is in recovery from an addiction should ever be prescribed another potential intoxicant is a remnant of the "all or none thinking" found in many 12-Step groups and programs. It is not based in fact. Yes, there may be a relative increase in risk, but the risk of true addiction to benzodiazepines (benzos), as opposed to development of tolerance and physical dependence, in an anxious patient is near zero in most people so the absolute risk is pretty low in someone with alcohol or opioid addiction. The same holds true for pain medication in alcohol dependent people. I try to balance risks and benefits as I do with any patient or treatment. The science tells us that, for most people, an addiction is specific to a drug, not to "addiction" or intoxication of any type. There is no such thing as an "addictive personality."

The other thing I'm impressed with is how poor any current pharmacotherapy is for chronic anxiety. The best treatment is good CBT (cognitive behavioral therapy), but it is hard to find and many patients are not good candidates (although they might be for skillful psychodynamic therapy). So I often find myself and the patient between a rock and a hard place.

For example, a patient who had childhood onset of moderate to severe anxiety, often starting with separation anxiety and school refusal. (Some patients report the onset of panic attacks before the age of ten). Most of these people are extremely anxious all of their lives and I see them because they have become alcohol dependent. I generally prescribe an antidepressant, an SSRI or SNRI, but these seem to have poor efficacy in these primary anxiety patients, as opposed to people with depression and anxiety together. In one recent patient, I stopped benzos and the patient got to the point where I thought, without relief, she would relapse to drinking. So I prescribed lorazepam and she almost immediately got much better, more stable, and with markedly reduced desire to drink. To my knowledge, she hasn't used benzos in an addictive fashion, although the other problems of tolerance and lack of long-term efficacy have not gone away. I usually try everything else I can: beta blockers, anticonvulsants, antidepressants, but rarely antipsychotics if nothing else works. I always prescribe relaxation training, breathing exercises, give patients information about mindfulness approaches, and also recommend a CBT workbook for anxiety. I may recommend seeing a therapist, but sometimes it's only benzos that seem to help.

Some years ago a colleague of mine studied vets with severe chronic PTSD who were on benzos, expecting their outcomes to be worse than others. Theirs were better than others. Now that may simply be due to this group being more stable/adherent so therefore benzos were continued. But still, where is the evidence in the published literature that shows that long-term benzo use is often damaging?

I worry that we prescribe truly toxic drugs like antipsychotics and depakote or lamotrigine to avoid benzos. Where is the evidence that many of these drugs actually help anxiety or are safe to treat it? I think there is a bias here – we withhold benzos (with very weak evidence of risk) and then – with no evidence of efficacy or safety, we prescribe toxic risky drugs instead. Make sense?

Also, underlying the bias is the pervasive idea, spread by many programs that 12-Step treatment or groups are 100% effective if the person just does as they're told. You and I both know that's absurd and untrue. Medicine frequently involves compromise between ideal and pragmatic goals, and balancing various risks and benefits.

Finally, there is fairly strong evidence that untreated insomnia, pain, and anxiety contribute substantially to increased relapse risk. It's easy to say "they should just tough it out or go to more meetings" but that seems pretty unreasonable and unsupportable to me. In the end, I view it as all coming down to outcomes. Is the patient better off? Are his or her symptoms less? Is he or she more functional? Does a prescription for benzos help the patient recover more fully? (Willenbring 2012)

Cannabis

Another common drug used for harm reduction is marijuana. Providing treatment to clients who do not embrace goals of abstinence often include continued use of cannabis. Many clients identify medicinal properties for marijuana use and most claim that it helps with anxiety/panic and pain management. They consider it safer than alcohol and other drugs and claim it helps them "stay away from the hard stuff".

Using cannabis as a substitute for alcohol is referred to as marijuana maintenance. The late Dr. Todd Mikuriya, MD was one of the first pioneers to use Medical Marijuana to treat alcohol dependence. Mikuriya prescribed medical marijuana to 92 patients who were suffering from severe alcohol dependence. One hundred percent of patients reported a major reduction in alcohol consumption and major reductions in alcohol-related harm. All reported that using medical marijuana caused far fewer life problems than did using alcohol.[21]

Many others agree that cannabis has medicinal value and according to the most recent (October 2011) Gallup poll, a record-high 50% of Americans now say the use of marijuana should be made legal, up from 46% last year. A Gallup survey last year (2010) found that 70% favored making it legal for doctors to prescribe marijuana in order to reduce pain and suffering.

In 1996, California became the first state in the union to allow for the medical use of marijuana. At the time of this writing, 15 more states and the District of Columbia have enacted similar laws. Some officials, including former U.S. Surgeon General Joycelyn Elders, have called for legalizing its use.

To be clear, I am not advocating that people smoke pot, but in the continuum of drug related harms, it is less harmful than most. In my thirty years of practice, I have observed many people who can use cannabis with few, if any, negative consequences. I have also worked with many people who have experienced severe psychosis from heavy use leading to hospitalization and treatment with anti-psychotic medication. I have also observed how heavy use has interfered with motivation, goal completion, concentration, and mood. Cannabis can be very potent and many people smoke way too much resulting in significant problems.

This chapter acknowledges that licit and illicit drug use is part of our world and chooses to work to minimize its harmful effects, and also acknowledges that some ways of using drugs are clearly safer than others. A common criticism of harm reduction programs is they allow people to use and do not provide active interventions. The following chapters detail an array of treatment activities used at Minnesota Alternatives and begin with a basic understanding of the nervous system.

---

[21] Mikuriya, T. H. (2004) *Cannabis as a Substitute for Alcohol: A Harm-Reduction Approach.* Journal of Cannabis Therapeutics. Vol. 4(1).

Chapter Three

Integration of Neuroscience into Treatment

The first two chapters identified the need for alternative approaches that are person-centered. The purpose of this chapter is to explain how neuroscience can aid the delivery of substance use treatment.

Due to advances in technology, we can now study the functional brain. Daily news reports share the latest findings: proteins causing Alzheimer's disease, stress causing holes in our brains, new insights into brain development, the discovery of new neurotransmitters, the impact of drugs and alcohol, and on and on.

Minnesota Alternatives integrates this science into the majority of the treatment process. The books *Evolve Your Brain* (J. Dispenza) and *The Practical Neuroscience of Buddha's Brain* (R. Hanson and R. Mendius) have served as useful resources for program development.

The clients have displayed strong enthusiasm and high levels of interest in brain science. They feel empowered by the knowledge and are equipped with effective skills and tools to manage difficult circumstances and improve the quality of their lives.

Key points that highlight brain science opportunities:

- We know that the brain is so powerful because it is extremely sensitive to experience.
- Where we place our attention defines us at a neurological level.
- We each have far more power to alter our brain, our behavior, and our personality than previously thought possible.
- Mindfulness practices have been shown to functionally disconnect the different regions of the brain that make up the "craving network".[22]
- A brain that is trained to a state of positivity is more functional than a brain in neutral, negative, or stress states.[23]

Understanding Our Nervous System

The purpose of this section is to provide a basic overview of how the nervous system works, some of the basic chemicals involved, and how the brain and body communicate.

---

[22] McGonigal, K. (2011) *How Mindfulness Makes the Brain Immune to Temptation.* The Science of Willpower.

[23] Achor, S. (2010) The Happiness Advantage. *The Seven Principles of Positive Psychology That Fuel Success and Performance at Work.*

The picture on the left shows all the nerves of the nervous system branching off the brain and the spinal cord. The picture on the right show how the nerves of the autonomic nervous system interact with the body's organs.

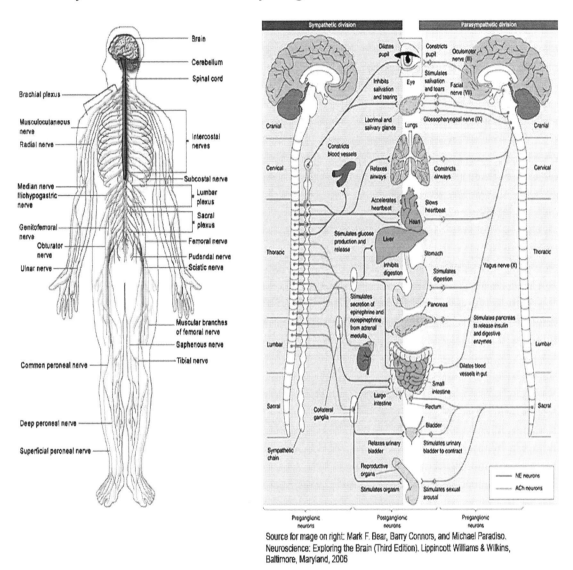

Source for image on right: Mark F. Bear, Barry Connors, and Michael Paradiso. Neuroscience: Exploring the Brain (Third Edition). Lippincott Williams & Wilkins, Baltimore, Maryland, 2006

The nervous system is the most important system in the body because it activates, controls, and coordinates all bodily functions. The other major systems in the body include: gastrointestinal, cardiovascular, digestive, dermal, lymphatic, muscular/skeletal, and reproductive.

The central nervous system (CNS) includes the brain and the spinal cord. The body receives information from the environment and sends it through nerves to the brain, and the brain in turns sends information back to the cells in the body. The other part of the nervous system is the peripheral nervous system (PNS) and it includes all nerves outside the brain and spinal cord. The PNS includes nerves that connect to tissues and organs and communicate to specific parts of the body through nerves that branch off the spinal cord.

Residing in both the central nervous system (brain and spinal cord) and the peripheral nervous system (all other nerves) is the autonomic (think automatic) nervous system. The autonomic nervous system interacts with all the other major systems in the body. It is controlled by the midbrain and is the body's automatic, self-regulating control system, regulating all the millions of processes we take for granted every day.

The autonomic nervous system is further divided into two types of nerve systems:

- Sympathetic nervous system: Mobilizes energy during times of stress and arousal. This is the "go system".
- Parasympathetic nervous system: Conserves energy and resources during relaxed states. This is the "stop system".

Here is a very important point:

The autonomic nervous system is intertwined with and helps regulate every other bodily system. Mental activity has greater direct influence over this system than any other system.

What does this mean? The autonomic nervous system can be influenced by mental activity and it interacts with all of our body's other systems. Mental activity can activate our go/arousal nerves or it can activate our stop/rest nerves. In other words, our thoughts can calm our nerves or our thoughts can excite them.

When teaching this essential point to clients, I demonstrate how one can willfully activate either system. I pound my fists on the table, while yelling obscenities, which causes arousal or sympathetic activation in not only me, but in others in the room. I then close my eyes, focus on deep breathing, and become fully present in the moment, noticing and describing the sensations I am experiencing in my body. I have now accessed the calming parasympathetic system.

Chronically high levels of arousal overwork the body's major organs/systems and result in overstimulation of the sympathetic nervous system (go system). This can then lead to an array of illnesses.

Conversely, when we stimulate the parasympathetic nervous system (stop system), calming, soothing, healing ripples spread through the body and brain. People can learn to calm themselves and tap into the parasympathetic wing of the nervous system by using:

- Diaphragmatic breathing
- Big exhalation
- Time inhalation to match exhalations
- Meditation
- Mindfulness
- Imagery

Take a deep breath and consider the reasons we should slow down. Modern times of autopilot, information overload, digital stimulation, stressful schedules, states of overwhelm, result in people living in elevated states of stress. According to a recently released Yale University study, stress causes the brain to shrink.

The next time you're stressed to the gills and cannot focus, think, or remember the ingredients for the meatloaf you make every week, you can legitimately blame stress.

"It's a short, easy story, actually," said neuroscientist and author David Eagleman. "Stress is underpinned by particular hormones that circulate through the body and the brain. Those stress hormones are very bad for brain tissue. They eat away at brain tissue. What's new to be stressed about is that stress is literally chewing miniature holes in your brain."

Not all stress poses a problem; our bodies are designed to combat stress by releasing the hormone cortisol. That response grew out of stresses such as, say, being chased by a tiger.

"The general story is that we evolved to have stress systems that are useful when you need a fast response," said Eagleman, director of the Laboratory for Perception and Action at the Baylor College of Medicine in Houston. "What we did not evolve for is chronic stress – that 21st-century stress that man and woman lives with."

Instead of a burst of stress hormones, most people have chronically elevated levels. "The body is simply not built to have high levels of stress for long periods," he said. "That's where the stuff eats away at your brain tissue."[24]

The ideal state of being is to keep the autonomic nervous system as a whole in balance. This means primarily parasympathetic activation for a baseline of ease and peacefulness, and mild sympathetic activation for enthusiasm, vitality, and passion, with occasional spikes in sympathetic to deal with demanding situations. The majority of clients identify symptoms of anxiety, so parasympathetic activation is a vital skill.

---

[24] Garcia, L. (2012) Dallas Morning News, *Stress Eats Holes in Your Brain.*

Nerve Cells (aka: Neurons)

The primary way the body and brain talk to each other is through nerves. The brain is made up of 75% water and glial cells (Greek word meaning glue) that play a supportive role for brain structure and function. Aside from water and glial cells, the brain primarily consists of nerve cells (neurons). Nerve cells consist of a cell body, cell nucleus, dendrites, and an axon.

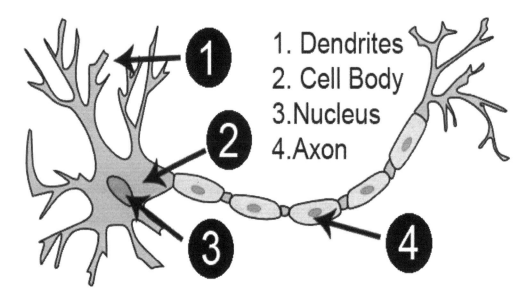

1. Dendrites
2. Cell Body
3. Nucleus
4. Axon

There are many types of neurons, and a tiny slice of brain tissue, the size of a grain of sand, contains about 100,000 nerve cells. Some nerve cells are much longer than brain neurons. Those that run from the brain down the spinal cord measure up to 3 feet.

Nerve cells are the most significant cells in the brain and the most fundamental component in our nervous system because they provide the pathway for communication. Nerve cells are the only cells in the body that communicate directly with one another sending messages back and forth in the form of electrochemical signals or impulses.

When passing information, neurons never actually touch each other; rather information is transmitted in the form of electrical impulses across the gaps that separate them, called synapses. A nerve cell fires or does not fire depending upon what chemicals (neurotransmitters) are present. These chemicals cross the synapse and influence the activity of the neighboring nerve cell. That in turn influences the next receiving neuron and so on. The chemicals sent from neuron to neuron fit into the receiving receptor's site much the same way a key fits into a lock.

See picture of neurons and synapse below:

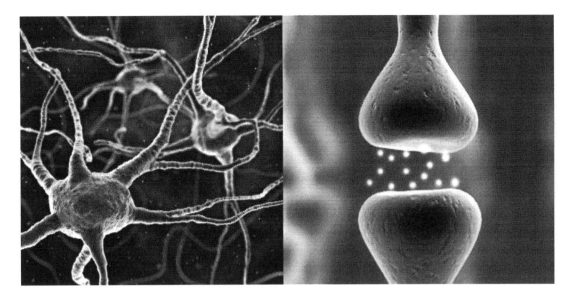

There are two fundamental types of neurotransmitters in the brain and nervous system – excitatory and inhibitory.

Excitatory neurotransmitters activate nerve transmission or allow the action potential in the next cell to be initiated. Inhibitory neurotransmitters inhibit or stop the activity in the next cell down the line. This is important to remember because in substance use disorders, the chemicals people take mimic our naturally occurring chemicals. Cocaine, for example, stimulates (excites) nerve transmission; while benzodiazepines slow (inhibit) transmission.

The primary neurotransmitters involved in drug and alcohol use include:

Dopamine – Is present in several parts of the brain and fuels attraction, focus, approach, wanting, and doing. Dopamine is responsible for feelings of pleasure.

Serotonin – Plays several complex roles in the brain and is widely distributed. One of the primary roles is regulating information flow by inhibiting the firing of neurons that might otherwise fire too quickly. Serotonin has broad implications in mood, sleep, appetite, and sexual functioning. It dampens, it paces, and it soothes.

Norepinephrine – Fuels alertness, arousal, excitement, and attention to sensory detail. It is one of the brain's natural stimulants responsible for the fight or flight reaction and part of the stress response.

Acetylcholine – Energizes all mental operations, consciousness, and thought itself. It transmits orders to the muscular system.

GABA (gamma-amino butyric acid) – Primarily works to inhibit the activity of neurons and calm electrical activity. It is the brain's natural Valium and suppresses over-excitement/anxiety while allowing higher cognitive processes to remain alert.

Glutamate – Is one of the primary stimulatory neurotransmitters. It is widely distributed in the brain and is engaged in many different activities.

Anandamide – Activates the group of cannabinoid receptors in different parts of the brain. Cannabinoid receptors are sensitive to tetrahydrocannabinol (THC), which mimics anandamide. Endocannabinoids serve as an internal neuromodulatory system and are involved in appetite, pain sensation, mood, memory, and synaptic plasticity.

Endorphins – Are related to pain perception and pain control. Release of endorphins not only decreases pain, but provide a sense of well-being and happiness.

To review, our body and brain communicate through our nervous system. The nervous system contains nerve cells. Nerve cells fire or do not fire depending upon what chemicals (neurotransmitters) are present. Some chemicals are stimulating whereas others stop action. Many of the neurotransmitters do not require any conscious action to activate, while others are determined by what we put in our bodies, what we are thinking and feeling, and how we are responding to our environments.

Three Brains in One

The brain is an example of the evolutionary development of humanity. The human brain has three evolutionary formations, the brain stem (hindbrain), the limbic system (midbrain), and the cerebral cortex (forebrain).

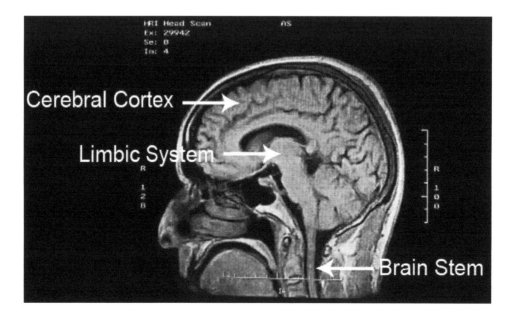

The **brainstem or (hindbrain)** was the first to evolve and includes the area where the spinal cord connects to the base of the brain. The brainstem supports basic life functions, including the maintenance and control of heart rate and breathing, swallowing, blood pressure, and various levels of wakefulness and sleep. Attached directly behind the brainstem is the cerebellum. The cerebellum has many functions and is a very active area of the brain. It plays a primary role in balance, coordination, and body movement, and facilitates automatic, hard-wired memories and behaviors.

The **middle brain (limbic system)** is located in the middle of the brain just above the brainstem and is about the size of an apricot. Although small in size, its influence on behavior is extensive, which is why it is also called the emotional brain. It is also referred to as the chemical brain because it is responsible for regulating many internal states. (Recall the autonomic nervous system is controlled by the midbrain.) In addition to the "automatic" regulatory functions, the midbrain controls vital functions for the preservation of life (fight or flight), helps to maintain homeostasis, and helps organize signals from our external world with our internal world. It is the meeting point for almost all nerves, connecting different parts of the brain as well as connecting the brain to the body. This part of the brain is the most hard-wired (more on what this means later) and is primarily composed of the thalamus, hypothalamus, pituitary, pineal gland, hippocampus, amygdala, and basal ganglia.

Our brain has its own **reward system** primarily located in the middle brain. The brain's reward system causes feelings of pleasure when it is "turned on" by something we enjoy, like eating good food, being in love, or using drugs/alcohol. The diagram below highlights the major structures of the reward system. It includes the ventral tegmental area (VTA), the nucleus accumbens, and the prefrontal cortex. Information travels from the VTA to the nucleus accumbens and then up to the prefrontal cortex. Although other brain structures are involved, this is the primary pathway activated by rewarding stimuli.

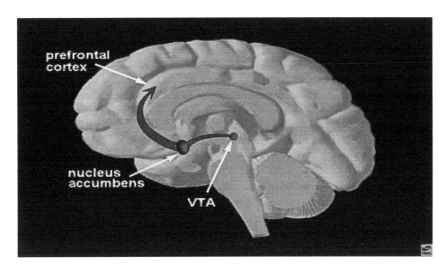

The **cerebral cortex (new/forebrain)** is the outer part of the brain that looks like a wrinkled sponge. Evolution's most sophisticated achievement to date, the forebrain, is the seat of our conscious awareness and is responsible for carrying out executive/higher functions like learning, remembering, creativity, invention, analyzing, and voluntary behavior. The neocortex (aside from the cerebellum) has more nerve cells than any other brain structure. Because the neocortex is the newest brain, it has fewer hard-wired programs and is more malleable since it facilitates our ability to think and choose differently.

Brain Development

Of all mammals, humans have the least mature brains at birth. In the period following birth, the human brain continues to grow at the same rate as in the womb. There are times in the first year of life when every second, multiple millions of nerve connections are established. Three-quarters of brain growth takes place outside the womb. By 3 years of age, the brain has reached 90% of its adult size; however the frontal lobe does not finish developing until the mid-twenties.[25]

In the early stages of life, the infant's brain has many more neurons and connections than necessary. Which connections survive the natural process of neural Darwinism depends largely upon input from the environment. An infant's early years have a significant impact on how the neurological networks that control human behavior will mature. To illustrate this, if a baby was kept in the dark for its first 5 years, despite perfectly good eyes at birth, the visual neurological units would not develop during the critical period allotted by nature, and irreversible blindness would result.

The three environmental conditions absolutely essential to optimal brain development are nutrition, physical security, and consistent emotional nurturing. Children need to be in an attachment relationship with at least one reliable, protective, psychologically, and reasonably non-stressed adult.[26] A further discussion regarding the importance of environmental influences will be discussed in the following chapter.

The completion of the frontal lobe is the last part of the brain to reach adult maturity. Again, the frontal lobe controls our impulses and our emotions. This helps explain why teenagers and young adults struggle with impulsive behavior. Drug and alcohol abuse before the mid-twenties is more dangerous, as the frontal lobe is still developing. Until recently, many scientists considered this stage of growth as the end of brain development,

---

[25] Shore, R. (1997) Citing data from Rethinking the Brain: New Insights into Early Development.
[26] Maté, G. (2010) *In the Realm of Hungry Ghosts.*

but we are not as rigid or hard-wired as science once speculated. Although the majority of brain development happens by our mid-twenties, the brain's advancement does not stop.

New brain cells can be generated in the hippocampus. We have the capacity to create more connections between different brain areas and produce natural brain nutrients, called neurotrophins, which can dramatically increase the size and complexity of nerve cell dendrites and also make surrounding cells stronger and more resistant. Certain parts of the brain are extremely neuroplastic. This means that by persistent learning, having new experiences, and modifying our behavior, we can continue to remold and shape the brain throughout our adult years.

Empowerment and Brain Opportunities

The harmful effects of substances cannot be overstated, and some chemicals have the power to temporarily "hijack" the brain. While some people abuse drugs or alcohol in ways that cause permanent brain damage, the majority of substance users are misled when they are taught that once they "cross the line" into dependence, they are now victims of an "out-of-control brain".

Minnesota Alternatives works to empower people by equipping them with knowledge and skills to learn how to self-regulate. **Self-regulation means maintaining a reasonably stable internal environment regardless of what is going on in the external environment.** The model emphasizes mindfulness and self-calming, and strives to teach people to "think greater than how they feel".

The brain is constantly reorganizing itself throughout the life span. Science shows that we have far more power to alter our brain, our behavior, and our personality than previously thought possible. How and where we place our attention, what we place our attention on, and for how long we place it define us at a neurological level. What flows through our mind sculpts our brain. If we think the same thoughts and behave in the same ways, our brain becomes hard-wired, the cells in the body become conditioned, and change becomes very difficult – especially as we age.[27]

Brain functioning involves both bottom-up processing and top-down processing. The more primitive brain areas (hindbrain and middle brain) involve bottom-up processing. They respond to external stimulation with automatic functions and do not involve conscious attention. This is very fast processing. The reward system is an example of bottom-up processing. It functions in the "here and now" and is constantly seeking reward (its evolutionary purpose is to ensure we eat and fornicate).

---

[27] Dispenza, J. (2007) *Evolve Your Brain: The Science of Changing Your Mind.*

The front part of the cerebral cortex (the frontal lobe which sits behind the forehead) is the seat of our conscious awareness, and is responsible for carrying out executive/higher functions. Engaging the frontal lobe involves top-down processing. It requires conscious, focused thought. It is slower than bottom-up processing, and is not an automatic function.

The frontal lobe is the command center, the CEO, the captain of the ship. When engaged, it has the capacity to quiet other parts of the brain, including the reward system. Teaching clients how to engage their frontal lobe helps them self-regulate and learn to make "executive" (vs. impulsive) decisions.

Strategies for Engaging the Frontal Lobe

Get out of survival mode. If we live in survival mode we have no extra energy to evolve and grow. We become more animal-like. Securing basic needs helps lay the foundation for personal growth.

Manage stress. Stress increases the value of immediate rewards or quick fixes. We are more likely to develop or engage in bad habits if under stress. When we live in a state of stress, we limit our potential for growth because the chemicals of stress make it more difficult to engage our "big thinking" frontal lobes.

Practice mindfulness. Mindfulness (being fully in the present) is an effective method to engage the frontal lobe and quiet the more primitive (reward) centers of the brain. Being fully in the moment allows us to be aware of our thoughts, feelings, body sensations, and our environments. Can we learn to observe and interrupt negative habitual thought processes?

Be intentional and use repetition. It takes many years to develop patterns of behavior or habits, and change does not happen overnight. Practice and repetition are essential to changing both our thoughts and our actions. Trying to change a behavior requires focused attention, and verbalizing our intentions helps to hold us accountable. People learn better by doing versus being told.

Practice mental rehearsal. This is a powerful way to grow and mold new circuits in our brain. If we involve all five senses and create vivid images of our new way of being, our new thoughts, feeling and behaviors, our brain does not know whether or not it is really happening. This prepares us for real life by practicing how to respond to difficult events before they occur. Practicing skills or new behaviors when we are centered and calm helps solidify them, and increases the likelihood of skillful "performance" when needed.

Engage in new or novel experiences. The brain needs new information to prevent it from becoming hard-wired and riddled with automatic programs of behavior. If we think the same things and behave in the same ways, and think the same things and behave in the same ways, and think the same things and behave in the same ways, change becomes very difficult. We are running on auto-pilot. Find ways to break routines and force ourselves to try new things. Make small, safe changes at first, and then as we become more comfortable with change, take more risks.

Enrich our life. Reward deficiency and lack of worthwhile opportunities increases the need for immediate gratification. When changing a behavior, build in rewards to satisfy the ever-hungry reward system. Even small positive actions every day increase dopamine and change neural structures that add to large changes over time. Laughter (even forced) neutralizes the negative effects of stress.

The "Happiness Advantage"

Shawn Achor spent more than a decade studying and researching the field of positive psychology at Harvard University and wrote a book called *The Happiness Advantage*.[28]

He suggests that we have the formula for happiness backwards – we chase it. We think if we accomplish this or that we will be happy, but instead we then change the bar for what is next. Work harder, get better grades, make more money, etc. Happiness sits behind our next accomplishment.

We have it backwards because science shows that if we train our brain to function in a positive state (instead of a stress, neutral, or negative state) it becomes 31% more productive. He also claims that only 25% of job success is related to our IQ whereas 75% of job success is from optimism level, social supports, and the ability to see stress as a challenge versus a threat. In other words, if we train our brain to a positive state, it works better, increasing our chance of success.

Dopamine is released by the following activities and dopamine not only makes us happy, it turns on the learning centers of the brain.

The *Happiness Advantage* proposes that the following activities, performed for 21 days, have been proven to re-wire the brain to a state of positivity:

- Identify three new things each day you are grateful for (retains a pattern that teaches you to scan the world for positives instead of negatives).

---

[28] Achor, S. (2010) The Happiness Advantage. *The Seven Principles of Positive Psychology That Fuel Success and Performance at Work.*

- Journal about one positive experience each day (allows the brain to re-experience it).

- Exercise (teaches us that behavior matters).

- Meditate (teaches us to focus our ADD [attention deficit disorder] brains that result from overstimulation and multi-tasking).

- Practice doing "random acts of kindness".

Interested in giving it a try?

Willpower

Self-control is an important consideration when treating addictions. Roy F. Baumeister, in his book (co-authored with John Tierney), *Willpower: Rediscovering the Greatest Human Strength*, describe the evidence behind what may seem like common-sense strategies to improve willpower. It includes the following highlights:[29]

- We have a finite amount of willpower that becomes depleted as we use it.

- We use the same stock of willpower for all manner of tasks.

- The same energy that is used for self-control is also used for making decisions. After making decisions, people perform worse at self-control. Conversely, after exerting self-control, decision-making shifts toward simpler and easier processes. For example: It is harder to resist temptations after a long day of making difficult decisions and we are at greater risk of losing our temper after a stressful day.

- Glucose plays an important role in self-control. Glucose is the chemical in the bloodstream that carries energy to the brain, muscles, and other organs and systems. In simple terms, glucose is fuel for the brain. Acts of self-control reduce blood glucose levels. Low levels of glucose predict poor performance on self-control tasks and tests. Replenishing glucose, even just with a glass of lemonade, improves self-control performance.

- Self-control can be strengthened. Engaging in some self-control activities for only a couple of weeks produces improvement. In one study, students were asked to watch their posture for a week. At the end of the week, those students performed better on self-control tasks – tasks that had nothing to do with sitting up straight – than students who had not been exercising control all week.

Strategies recommended for improved self-control include:

- Be proactive and try to avoid positions requiring stressful decisions. For example, allow enough time for a project or get the car fixed before it breaks down.

- Start each day with a full supply of willpower by getting a good night's sleep and eating a nutritious breakfast.

---

[29] Baumeister, R., Tierney, J. (2011) *Willpower: Rediscovering the Greatest Human Strength. (p. 238-260).*

- Maintain adequate glucose levels.

- Avoid making binding decisions when our energy is down, because we will tend to favor choices with short-term gains and delayed costs.

- Avoid changing multiple behaviors or accomplishing many goals at once, and instead, focus attention to one area. If needed, establish a plan to address other areas in the future, because having a plan allows the unconscious to quit fretting.

- Keep our environments neat as order is contagious.

- Self-monitor progress and reward ourselves when we accomplish goals.

This chapter has identified many opportunities neuroscience and other strategies offer for the delivery of addiction treatment. Before discussing how these activities can be integrated in a program setting, the next chapter will discuss the critical role of environmental influences, the brains response to drugs and alcohol, withdrawal and alcohol considerations, and a brief section about medications commonly used for the treatment of addictions.

Chapter Four

Environmental and Chemical Influences

Addiction is not an equal opportunity experience.

The previous chapter discussed the opportunities for positive change through understanding brain functions and brain training. In addition to understanding the opportunities, it is important to also discuss the risks posed by unhealthy environments, stress, trauma, and abuse of drugs and/or alcohol. This chapter also includes information on withdrawal and pharmacological interventions.

Environmental Influences

Most people try alcohol and/or drugs but do not go on to become addicted. Research has reinforced the idea that mere exposure will lead to addiction, because most lab animals can be induced into compulsive self-administration of drugs and alcohol. The experience of caged animals does not represent the lives of free animals, including human beings.

Dr. Alexander at Simon Fraser University in British Columbia[30] conducted experiments to show that even lab rats, given reasonable living situations, will resist the addictive appeal of drugs. He went on to demonstrate that in a "natural" environment, a rat will stay away from morphine if given a choice, even if it's already physically dependent on the narcotic. "Nothing we tried", reported Alexander, "instilled a strong appetite for morphine or produced anything that looked like addiction in rats that were housed in a reasonably normal environment".

The intersection of environment and brain function was highlighted in an interesting study that found that adult monkeys raised in private cages developed pronounced changes in brain dopamine systems when they were transferred to group cages. The social status of the primates greatly determined the types of brain changes that occurred. Lower-ranking monkeys became much more inclined to self-administer intravenous cocaine when it was made available to them. The more dominant ones showed no such increase in craving for cocaine.[31]

---

[30] Rat Park was a study into drug addiction conducted in the late 1970s (and published in 1980), by Canadian psychologist Bruce K. Alexander and his colleagues at Simon Fraser University in British Columbia, Canada.

[31] Morgan et al. (2002) Social dominance in monkeys: dopamine D_2 receptors and cocaine self-administration, *Nature Neuroscience* 5, 169 – 174.

Another example of how stressful environments impact behavior can be found in a study that discovered that seven out of eight soldiers addicted to heroin in Vietnam quit using heroin on their own when they returned to the United States (Robin, L. 1980).[32]

The well-known Adverse Childhood Experience (ACE) Study[33] looked at 10 separate categories of painful experiences (including family violence, parental divorce, drug or alcohol abuse in the family, death of a parent, and physical and sexual abuse) in thousands of people. For each adverse childhood experience or ACE, the risk for early initiation of substance abuse increased 2 to 4 times. Subjects with 5 or more ACE's had 7 to 10 times greater risk for substance abuse than those with none.

Up to two-thirds of men and women in substance abuse treatment report childhood abuse & neglect and 50% of women in substance abuse treatment have a history of rape or incest.[34] Treatment providers must practice Trauma-Informed Care (see Chapter 5).

The book, *In the Realm of Hungry Ghosts* by Dr. Gabor Maté, provides an excellent summary of the nature of addiction and he concludes that three factors need to coincide for substance addiction to occur: a susceptible organism, a drug with addictive potential, and stress.

The Concept of Attunement

In his book, Maté also introduces the concept of attunement.[35] Attunement literally means being "in tune" with someone else's emotional states. It is not a question of parental love, but of the parent's ability to be present emotionally in such a way that the infant or child feels understood, accepted, and mirrored. Attunement is the real language of love, the conduit by which a preverbal child can realize that he/she is loved. It is deeply instinctive and easily subverted when the parent is stressed, depressed, or distracted. Attunement is especially likely to be lacking if parents missed out on it in their own childhoods.

Poorly attuned relationships provide an inadequate template for the development of the child's neurological and psychological self-regulation systems.

---

[32] Robin, L. N., Helzer, J. E., Hesselbrock, M., Wish, E. (1980). Vietnam veterans three years after Vietnam: How our study changed our view of heroin, *Yearbook of substance use and abuse.* New York: Human Science Press.

[33] *American Journal of Preventive Medicine* (1998) Volume 14, Issue 4 , Relationship of Childhood Abuse and Household Dysfunction to Many of the Leading Causes of Death in Adults: The Adverse Childhood Experiences (ACE) Study.

[34] Governor's Commission on Sexual and Domestic Violence (2006) Commonwealth of MA.

[35] Maté, G. (2010) *In the Realm of Hungry Ghosts (pages 249-254).*

This strikes me as a very important concept, and when discussed with clients, they have a strong identification and emotional response, often causing tearfulness. They frequently report childhood experiences of chaos, absent or impaired parents, and/or overt abuse.

When engaged with clients in a deeply supportive and emotionally present way, this concept of attunement can be used to help them feel calm, connected, valued, and cared for. This may provide them "a reason to live", and may motivate them to reduce or stop their use of substances. When they understand attunement, it also provides a powerful incentive to "show up" for the children or other important people in their lives. For example, a client with a long history of heroin addiction is now functioning as the primary caregiver for her 11-year-old brother because their mother is "distracted". She is "tuned in" to him, and this role provides her a very strong reason to stay well and present in his life.

Are children increasingly at risk of not experiencing attunement because their parents are distracted by their computers or "smart" phones?

Dr. Kevin Turnquist summarizes:

"Enlightened systems of the future will emphasize the creation of optimal environments for our children to develop in, from the womb right up through adulthood. We'll have to attend to all of the needs of developing nervous systems starting by providing pregnant moms with safe, secure environments to carry their kids in, good nutrition, and excellent obstetrical care, and helping them keep free of preventable stresses."

"We can't park our kids in front of flickering screens for hours on end and expect that they'll develop good brains as a result. To develop optimally functioning brains, our children need physical exercise and a wide variety of stimulating mental activities. They have to receive all of the essential building blocks for healthy brains in their diets. They have to be free from abuse and other stresses that their developing nervous systems aren't equipped to handle. And, most of all, they must be raised in the presence of loving, empathic caretakers who spend enough time with them. Empathy and love are every bit as crucial for the development of a stable sense of self as any measurable variable that we can come up with."

The Brain's Response to Drugs and Alcohol

Neuroscientists have learned a great deal about how drugs of abuse affect our central nervous system and exert their influence. Abused drugs alter the way neurotransmitters carry their message from neuron to neuron. Some drugs mimic neurotransmitters, whereas others block them. Still others alter the way neurotransmitters are released or activated. Ultimately, in all cases, the brain's reward system is affected; however, addiction requires more than activation of the reward system. Drugs can change the brain of susceptible individuals in complex ways that include both the reward system as well as brain regions involved in executive functions and judgment.

Variables that contribute to use include genetic susceptibility, environmental factors, characteristics of drugs themselves, and stress or other emotional issues.

The following information comes from NIDA:[36]

How do drugs work in the brain?

Drugs are chemicals. They work in the brain by tapping into the brain's communication system and interfering with the way nerve cells normally send, receive, and process information. Some drugs, such as marijuana and heroin, can activate neurons because their chemical structure mimics that of a natural neurotransmitter. This similarity in structure "fools" receptors and allows the drugs to lock onto and activate the nerve cells. Although these drugs mimic brain chemicals, they don't activate nerve cells in the same way as a natural neurotransmitter, which leads to abnormal messages being transmitted through the network.

Other drugs, such as amphetamines or cocaine, can cause the nerve cells to release abnormally large amounts of natural neurotransmitters or prevent the normal recycling of these brain chemicals. This disruption produces a greatly amplified message, ultimately disrupting communication channels. The difference in effect can be described as the difference between someone whispering into your ear and someone shouting into a microphone.

How do drugs work in the brain to produce pleasure?

Most drugs of abuse directly or indirectly target the brain's reward system by flooding the circuit with dopamine. Dopamine is a neurotransmitter present in regions of the brain that regulate movement, emotion, cognition, motivation, and feelings of pleasure. The overstimulation of this system, which rewards our natural behaviors, produces the euphoric effects sought by people who abuse drugs and teaches them to repeat the behavior.

How does stimulation of the brain's pleasure circuit teach us to keep taking drugs?

Our brains are wired to ensure that we will repeat life-sustaining activities by associating those activities with pleasure or reward. Whenever this reward circuit is activated, the brain notes that something important is happening that needs to be remembered, and

---

[36] National Institute of Drug Abuse (2009) *Drugs, Brains, and Behavior: The Science of Addiction.*

teaches us to do it again and again, without thinking about it. Because drugs of abuse stimulate the same circuit, we learn to abuse drugs in the same way.

Why are drugs more addictive than natural rewards?

When some drugs of abuse are taken, they can release 2 to 10 times the amount of dopamine that natural rewards do. In some cases, this occurs almost immediately (as when drugs are smoked or injected), and the effects can last much longer than those produced by natural rewards. The resulting effects on the brain's pleasure circuit dwarfs those produced by naturally rewarding behaviors such as eating and sex. The effect of such a powerful reward strongly motivates people to take drugs again and again. This is why scientists sometimes say that drug abuse is something we learn to do very, very well.

What happens to your brain if you keep taking drugs?

Just as we turn down the volume on a radio that is too loud, the brain adjusts to the overwhelming surges in dopamine (and other neurotransmitters) by producing less dopamine or by reducing the number of receptors that can receive signals. As a result, dopamine's impact on the reward circuit of a drug abuser's brain can become abnormally low, and the ability to experience any pleasure is reduced. This is why the abuser eventually feels flat, lifeless, and depressed, and is unable to enjoy things that previously brought him or her pleasure. Now, the abuser needs to take drugs just to try and bring the dopamine function back up to normal. And, a larger amount of the drug is required to create the dopamine high. This is an effect known as tolerance.

How does long-term drug taking affect brain circuits?

We know that the same sort of mechanisms involved in the development of tolerance can eventually lead to profound changes in neurons and brain circuits, with the potential to severely compromise the long-term health of the brain. For example, glutamate is another neurotransmitter that influences the reward circuit and the ability to learn. When the optimal concentration of glutamate is altered by drug abuse, the brain attempts to compensate for this change, which can cause impairment in cognitive function. Similarly, long-term drug abuse can trigger adaptations in habit or unconscious memory systems. Conditioning is one example of this type of learning, whereby environmental cues become associated with the drug experience and can trigger cravings if the individual is later exposed to these cues, even without the drug itself being available. This learned "reflex" is extremely robust and can emerge even after many years of abstinence.

What other brain changes occur with abuse?

Chronic exposure to drugs of abuse disrupts the way critical brain structures interact to control and inhibit behaviors related to drug abuse. Just as continued abuse may lead to tolerance or the need for higher drug dosages to produce an effect, it may also lead to addiction, which can drive an abuser to seek out and take drugs compulsively. Drug addiction erodes a person's self-control and ability to make sound decisions, while sending intense impulses to take drugs (NIDA).

Clients find education about how drugs and alcohol impact the brain very enlightening. Their light bulbs turn on when they learn that excessive dopamine can destroy essential receptors, or when taking drugs that block transmission, the brain responds by creating more receptors. When they are told that some drugs (dissociatives for example) prevent their midbrain from connecting to the frontal lobe, they really wake up. Why would you want your brain to function from your primitive midbrain, and cut off your access to reasoning and judgment?

Effects on Neurotransmitters[37]

Methamphetamine – Meth is the strongest of all stimulant drugs. It is chemically similar to dopamine. This similarity allows methamphetamine to fool the dopamine transporter into carrying methamphetamine to the nerve terminal. Methamphetamine also directly crosses nerve cell membranes, and once inside nerve terminals, it enters dopamine vesicles and causes the release of dopamine. The result is a high concentration of dopamine in the synapse activating and activating over and over. Norepinephrine and serotonin levels also become elevated in the synapse. It differs from cocaine in that it can damage neurons in frontal cortex, amygdala, and striatum (brain region involved in movement). The message of meth is that goals do not matter anymore. When engorged on dopamine, the ventral striatum acts as if it is pursuing goals, yet there are not goals.[38] Long-term use is associated with symptoms that mirror Parkinson's disease of tremors, rigidity, balance and posture, and motor difficulties.

Cocaine – Cocaine blocks the dopamine from leaving the synaptic gaps (prevents the reuptake) between the brain's neurons, and this leads to a buildup of dopamine; the brain thus remains stimulated. Users often take cocaine in "binges," during which the cocaine is used repeatedly and at increasingly higher doses. This can lead to increased irritability, restlessness, panic attacks, and paranoia/psychosis. With increasing dosages or frequency of use, the risk of adverse psychological or physiological effects increases.

---

[37] National Institute of Drug Abuse (2009) *Drugs, Brains, and Behavior: The Science of Addiction.*

[38] Lewis, M. (2011) *Memoirs of an Addicted Brain.*

Opiates – Opioid receptors are normally activated by endogenous neural endorphin chemicals. Heroin saturates these opioid receptors and creates euphoria. Opiate receptors are widely distributed in the brain and body. Opiates provide a calming feeling by inhibiting neurons activated by pain or stress and they also increase the flow of dopamine in the ventral striatum creating feelings of pleasure. Opiates relieve pain by blocking the transmission of pain messages between neurons and therefore prevent pain messages from reaching the brain (known as analgesia). Heroin penetrates the brain more quickly than other opiates. There are lots of opiate receptors on the brain stem, which controls breathing and misuse can result in accidental overdose.

Speedballing (alternatively known as powerballing) is a term commonly referring to the intravenous use of cocaine with heroin or morphine in the same syringe. The term can also be applied to use of pharmaceutical opioids, benzodiazepines, or barbiturates along with amphetamine derivatives. This cocktail of drugs can cause a strong physical dependence and withdrawal symptoms. Cocaine acts as a stimulant, whereas heroin/morphine acts as a depressant. Co-administration provides an intense rush of euphoria with a high that is supposed to combine the effects of both drugs, while hoping to reduce the negative effects, such as anxiety and sedation. In general, the combined use with cocaine is done to avoid the sedative effect of heroin. Mixing a depressant with a stimulant causes a state of general confusion, incoherence, blurred vision, stupor, and drowsiness. The combination can result in uncontrolled and uncoordinated motor skills, with the risk of excessive arousal and death. There may be paranoid delusions, as well as intense depression, and hallucinations.[39]

Alcohol – Alcohol has a widespread impact on the brain and impacts multiple neurotransmitters. Alcohol affects judgment, emotion, breathing/heart rate, and balance/coordination. Alcohol promotes GABA (gamma-amino butyric acid), a neurotransmitter that primarily works to inhibit the activity of neurons. Similarly, alcohol may inhibit/block release of the excitatory neurotransmitter glutamate. Some evidence suggests that alcohol may activate naturally occurring opioid and cannabinoid pathways. Alcohol enhances the functioning of GABA, but long-term use results in "rebound", causing a risk for seizure/heart attack if not slowly tapered. Benzodiazepines work on GABA so they are often used to aid symptoms of withdrawal.

Hypnotics – Hypnotics (prescription sleeping pills, benzodiazepines, barbiturates) binds to a subtype of GABA receptor. Again, GABA is a neurotransmitter that primarily works to inhibit the activity of neurons. When hypnotics bind to this receptor, it slows and stops activity in certain parts of the brain, especially parts that are responsible for processing thoughts.

---

[39] Wiley-Interscience (2007) *Healing Addiction: An Integrated Pharmacopsychosocial Approach to Treatment,* p. 122.

Marijuana – Anandamide is an endogenous (naturally occurring) cannabinoid neurotransmitter, which activates cannabinoid receptors in different parts of the brain. Endocannabanoids serve as an internal neuromodulatory system with at least five identified members. They are involved in appetite, pain sensation, mood, memory, and synaptic plasticity. Marijuana (THC) mimics anandamide and activates these internal receptors.

Endocannabinoids are released just after neurons have fired, and in some parts of the brain, increase the firing rate of the neuron that just released them. By increasing the action of the neurons that are already active, cannabinoids cause each thought, each response, each act of perception or imagination, to magnify itself. This is what produces mental exploration when "high" but misses the "big picture" due to being so caught up in the momentum of the present reflection.[40] Some brain areas have many cannabinoid receptors, while others have few or none. In low to medium doses, marijuana can cause relaxation, reduced coordination, reduced blood pressure, sleepiness, disruption in attention, and an altered sense of time. In high doses, marijuana can cause paranoia, impaired memory, and disorientation.

Dissociatives – DXM (dextromethorphan, found in cough syrup), ketamine, PCP – (phencyclidine, also known as angel dust), glue, and gasoline are all drugs that dissociate feelings from reality. These chemical block the NMDA (N-methyl-D-aspartate) receptors, which are fundamental agents of synaptic plasticity (which facilitate neural connections and learning). When NMDA receptors are blocked, "reality" stops getting through. A well-functioning brain synchronizes limbic (midbrain) meaning with the sense of the cerebral cortex and constantly flows in both directions. Dissociatives close down the cortico-limbic bridge so the limbic system is no longer constrained by the logic and reasoning of the cerebral cortex.[41] Long-term use results in memory loss and speech difficulties.

Hallucinogens – LSD (lysergic acid diethylamide) looks just like serotonin molecules and therefore binds tightly to serotonin receptors. Once encamped in the receptors, LSD prevents the inhibitory, soothing, filtering, and regulating role of serotonin. The brain now responds to everything, including the tiniest fragments of thought and perception resulting in information overload. [42] The brain loses its ability to integrate information causing widespread effects including emotional swings, altered perceptions, delusions, and visual hallucinations.

---

[40] Lewis, M. (2011) *Memoirs of an Addicted Brain.*
[41] Lewis, M. (2011) *Memoirs of an Addicted Brain.*
[42] Lewis, M. (2011) *Memoirs of an Addicted Brain.*

Ecstasy – MDMA (3,4-methylenedioxy-N-methylamphetamine) causes neurons to release greater amounts of serotonin and dopamine than normal. MDMA can cause damage to serotonin-containing neurons. MDMA can cause liver problems in certain cases.

Synthetic or Designer Drugs

Designer drugs are drugs that are created to avoid the provisions of existing drug laws, usually by preparing analogs or derivatives of existing drugs by modifying their chemical structure to varying degrees, or less commonly by finding drugs with entirely different chemical structures that produce similar subjective effects to illegal recreational drugs.

Synthetic marijuana (often known as "K2" or "Spice") is often sold in legal retail outlets as "herbal incense" and labeled "not for human consumption" to mask its intended purpose and to avoid Food and Drug Administration (FDA) regulatory oversight of the manufacturing process.

Synthetic cannabinoids are chemically engineered substances similar to THC, the active ingredient in marijuana. When smoked or ingested, synthetic cannabinoids can produce a high similar to marijuana. Initially developed for pain management research and the effects of cannabis on the brain, these substances have recently become popular alternatives to marijuana.[43]

The less desirable effects of synthetic marijuana include agitation, extreme nervousness, nausea, vomiting, tachycardia (fast, racing heartbeat), elevated blood pressure, tremors and seizures, hallucinations, and dilated pupils. The absence of an antipsychotic chemical, found in natural cannabis, may make synthetic cannabis more likely to induce psychosis than natural cannabis.

Research on the safety of synthetic cannabis is only now becoming available. Initial studies are focused on the role of synthetic cannabis and psychosis. It seems likely that synthetic cannabis can precipitate psychosis and in some cases, it is prolonged. These studies suggest that synthetic cannabinoid intoxication is associated with acute psychosis, worsening of previously stable psychotic disorders, and also may have the ability to trigger a chronic (long-term) psychotic disorder among vulnerable individuals such as those with a family history of mental illness.[44]

---

[43] Sigillata, T., (2010) *What's the buzz?: Synthetic marijuana, K2, Spice*, JWH-018 : Scienceblogs.com. Retrieved November 24, 2010.

[44] Brauser, D., *Medscape Medical News, Psychiatry*, "Synthetic Cannabis May Pose an Even Greater Psychosis Risk".

Professor John W. Huffman, who first synthesized many of the cannabinoids used in synthetic cannabis, is quoted as saying, "People who use it are idiots, and you don't know what it's going to do to you".[45]

Use of synthetic marijuana is alarmingly high. According to data from the 2011 Monitoring the Future survey of youth drug-use trends, 11.4 % of 12th graders used Spice or K2 in the past year, making it the second most commonly used illicit drug among seniors.

Substituted Cathinones ("Bath Salts")

"Bath salts," are derivatives of cathinone. Cathinone is found in the shrub Catha edulis (khat). The four most widely recognized substituted cathinones are mephedrone, methylenedioxypyrovalerone (MDPV), a psychoactive drug with stimulant properties, which acts as a norepinephrine-dopamine reuptake inhibitor (NDRI), methylone, and methedrone. Bath salts come in the form of tablets or a powder, which users can swallow, snort or inject, producing similar effects to MDMA, amphetamines, and cocaine.

Similar to the adverse effects of cocaine, LSD, and methamphetamine, bath salt use is associated with increased heart rate and blood pressure, extreme paranoia, hallucinations, and violent behavior, which may cause users to harm themselves or others.[46]

An article highlights this concern:

"Doctors worry that users who repeatedly abuse bath salts could suffer long-term damage."

"Alex Seaton is haunted by that idea. Sitting in the Washington County jail, Seaton said voices were still speaking to him 10 weeks after an arrest ended his binge of bath salt use this summer."

"'I'm definitely hearing stuff,' he said in August, sitting in a jail visiting room with a robe hanging from his thin frame."

"Seaton, 19, said he had done various drugs in the past few years, but switched to bath salts because they were legal at the time. He needed to pass drug screenings as he searched for a job, he said."

"At first, Seaton said, bath salts made him feel good and talkative. The more he and a friend snorted, the worse things got."

---

[45] *Live Science*, "Fake Weed, Real Drug: K2 Causing Hallucinations in Teens". Retrieved November 24, 2010.

[46] Coppola, M., Mondola, R. (2012) *Toxicology Letters* 211 (2): 144–149, "Synthetic cathinones: Chemistry, pharmacology and toxicology of a new class of designer drugs of abuse marketed as 'bath salts' or 'plant food'".

"He began thinking the government spoke to him through audio speakers. He saw shadow people. He couldn't stop taking the drugs, constantly thinking, 'I wanted more, more, more, more, more,' he said. Seaton snorted them in heavy doses for a couple of months and wound up in the psychiatric unit of a hospital."

"His older brother, Nick Seaton, saw the change in Alex: 'It seems like the bath salts specifically put him over the edge.'"

"The low point came when Seaton's parents were away this summer. He broke into their Cottage Grove house and surrounded himself with loaded guns, according to court documents. Witnesses heard shots one afternoon. Seaton told officers that 'voices' made him do it to prevent an alien invasion."

"'This stuff is definitely screwing my head,' Seaton said during the interview at the county jail, his eyes wide under a mop of shaggy brown hair. 'I've never heard voices in my freakin' life until this bath salt.'" [47]

President Barack Obama signed a bill into law in July 2012 that bans the sale, production and possession of more than two dozen of the most common bath salt drugs. But health professionals say lawmakers cannot keep pace with bath salt producers, who constantly adjust their chemical formulations to come up with new synthetic drugs that aren't covered by new laws. Experts who have studied the problem estimate there are more than 100 different bath salt chemicals in circulation.

"The moment you start to regulate one of them, they'll come out with a variant that sometimes is even more potent," said Nora Volkow, director of the National Institute on Drug Abuse.

Mixing Drugs/Alcohol

When drugs/alcohol are combined, there are three possible effects:

- **They act independently of one another.** For example, alcohol does not seem to interfere with vitamins or oral contraceptives (birth control pills), or vice versa.
- **They can increase each other's effects.** This could happen because they affect the brain in the same way or because one drug increases the concentration of the other in the body. For instance, alcohol and antihistamines are both central nervous system depressants. Mixing them can make both the wanted effects of the drugs (e.g., decreasing self-consciousness) as well as the side effects (e.g., drowsiness)

---

[47] Louwagie, P. (2011) *Star Tribune*, *"Bath salts hit U.S. 'like a freight train'"*

stronger. Some drugs become more dangerous when they are mixed because their effects are compounded, increasing the risk of side effects or overdose.

- **They can decrease each other's intended effects.** This occurs when one drug "blocks" or prevents another drug from working. It could also happen when two drugs have opposite effects on the brain (e.g., drowsiness caused by alcohol versus alertness caused by caffeine). When prescription medication is mixed with other drugs or alcohol, the medication may not work as it should.

There is always some danger associated with mixing drugs, but the actual risks involved depend on the kind of drugs being combined and the amounts being used. Alcohol is perhaps most often mixed with other drugs and it is also among the most dangerous when combined with other substances.

The most common harmful effects of mixing drugs are:

- Central nervous system depression, which can range from drowsiness (at its mildest) to coma (at its most severe)
- Respiratory depression, which can lead to a person not breathing/death
- Cardiac effects, such as changes in heart rhythm that can lead to the heart stopping
- Decreased seizure threshold, meaning that the brain can have a seizure more easily
- Psychiatric effects such as psychosis

Withdrawal Information

Withdrawal effects are usually the opposite of the intoxicating effects. This means if someone uses stimulants for energy, the withdrawal symptoms include an energy crash/extreme fatigue. If someone uses inhibitory or calming chemicals, withdrawal will include anxiety, insomnia, and restlessness. These opposite effects are often the reason people return to using.

Withdrawal symptoms vary depending upon the person and the chemicals involved. Although withdrawal can be uncomfortable and painful, medical risks are primarily associated with alcohol and the sedatives/hypnotics (prescription sleeping pills, benzodiazepines, barbiturates).

Alcohol: Withdrawal can be very dangerous and death can occur due to risk of seizures and heart attacks. Withdrawal process should include medical oversight.

- Sweating
- Feeling nauseated or vomiting
- Racing heart

- Hands shaking
- Feeling agitated or anxious
- Trouble sleeping
- Fever
- Increased blood pressure
- Headache
- Heartburn

Hypnotics: Includes prescription sleeping pills, benzodiazepines, and barbiturates. Detox requires slow titration and medical oversight. Rapid withdrawal can cause psychosis, convulsions, and severe anxiety.

- Sweating or increased pulse rate
- Increased hand tremor
- Insomnia
- Nausea or vomiting
- Transient visual, tactile, or auditory hallucinations or illusions
- Anxiety
- Grandmal seizures

Stimulants/Cocaine: Medical detox not needed but withdrawal can be very uncomfortable. The initial crash involves agitation, depression, and intense craving. Within days, people experience fatigue, low energy, and decreased interest. Episodic craving and dysphoric (unpleasant) mood can last for weeks.

Opiates (morphine, codeine, oxycodone, heroin): Very uncomfortable withdrawal but medical detox is not necessary. A secure facility can provide support to get through the acute experience.

- Increased pain sensitivity
- Pupillary dilation/runny eyes
- Dysphoric (unpleasant) mood
- Stomach cramps/diarrhea
- Severe muscle and bone aches
- Yawning
- Insomnia

- Nausea or vomiting
- Fever/sweating

Overdose Information[48]

Deaths from overdose are most common for people with a history of chronic use or after a period of abstinence. Therefore people coming out of treatment, detox, or incarceration are particularly vulnerable.

- The majority of overdoses occur when a user combines opioids with depressants such as alcohol, benzodiazepines, and tricyclic antidepressants.
- Persons who have had an overdose in the past are also at an increased risk of future overdoses.
- Factors that increase risk are reduced tolerance, mixing drugs, and using alone as friends can intervene if they observe an overdose.
- Opioid overdose leads to death by respiratory depression which usually takes 1 to 3 hours. Remember there are a high number of opiate receptors on the brain stem, which controls breathing.

Heroin overdose can be quickly and safely reversed through the injection of Naloxone [brand name Narcan], a prescription drug used to revive persons who have overdosed on heroin or other opioids. Naloxone, an opiate antagonist, has long been administered by doctors and paramedics during emergency resuscitation after an opiate overdose and use of Naloxone by drug users is a new and innovative approach to reducing opiate-related mortality.

Alcohol Considerations[49]

Alcohol or ethyl alcohol (ethanol) refers to the intoxicating ingredient found in wine, beer and hard liquor. Ethanol is a volatile, flammable, colorless liquid with psychoactive properties. It is also used in thermometers, as a solvent, and as a fuel. Alcohol arises naturally from carbohydrates when certain micro-organisms metabolize them in the absence of oxygen, called fermentation.

Beer, wine, and other liquor contain different amounts of alcohol. The amount of alcohol in distilled liquor is known as proof. Proof refers to the amount of alcohol in the liquor; for example, 100-proof liquor contains 50% alcohol, 40-proof liquor contains 20% alcohol, and

---

[48] Harm Reduction Coalition.

[49] The National Council on Alcoholism and Drug Dependence.

so on. Traditional wine has approximately 8 to 14% alcohol, while regular beer has 4 to 6% alcohol.

Recent studies show that moderate use of alcohol may have a beneficial effect on the coronary system. In general, for healthy people, one drink per day for women and no more than two drinks per day for men would be considered the maximum amount of alcohol consumption to be considered low-risk use. However, the amount of alcohol that a person can drink safely is highly individual, depending on genetics, age, sex, weight, and family history. A drink is considered to be:

- 4-5 ounces of wine
- 10 ounces of wine cooler
- 12 ounces of beer
- 1-1/4 ounces of distilled liquor (80 proof)

How Alcohol Travels Through the Body

Alcohol is metabolized extremely quickly by the body. Unlike foods, which require time for digestion, alcohol needs no digestion and is quickly absorbed. Alcohol gets "special treatment" in the body absorbing and metabolizing before most other nutrients. About 20% is absorbed directly across the walls of an empty stomach and can reach the brain within 1 minute.

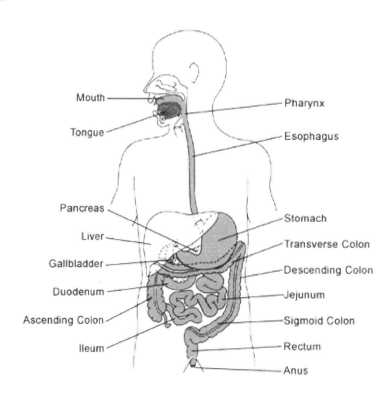

Once alcohol reaches the stomach, it begins to break down with the alcohol dehydrogenase enzyme. This process reduces the amount of alcohol entering the blood by approximately 20%. (Women produce less of this enzyme, which partially explains why women become more intoxicated on less alcohol than men.) In addition, about 10% of alcohol is expelled in the breath and urine.

Alcohol is rapidly absorbed in the upper portion of the small intestine. The alcohol-laden blood then travels to the liver via the veins and capillaries of the digestive tract, which affects nearly every liver cell. The liver cells are the only cells in our body that can produce enough of the enzyme alcohol dehydrogenase to oxidize alcohol at an appreciable rate.

Though alcohol affects every organ of the body, its most dramatic impact is on the liver. The liver cells normally prefer fatty acids as fuel, and package excess fatty acids as triglycerides, which they then route to other tissues of the body. However, when alcohol is present, the liver cells are forced to first metabolize the alcohol, letting the fatty acids accumulate, sometimes in huge amounts. Alcohol impairs the liver's ability to metabolize fats. This explains why heavy drinkers tend to develop fatty livers.

The liver is able to metabolize approximately one drink per hour. If more alcohol arrives in the liver than the enzymes can handle, the excess alcohol travels to all parts of the body, circulating until the liver enzymes are finally able to process it.

The following sections describe serious medical complications that people with severe alcohol dependence may experience.

Alcohol-Related Medical Complications

Fatty Liver and Liver Disease

With moderate drinking, the liver can process alcohol fairly safely. However, heavy drinking overtaxes the liver resulting in serious consequences. A liver clogged with fat causes liver cells to become less efficient at performing their necessary tasks, resulting in impairment of a person's nutritional health. Fatty liver is the first stage of liver deterioration in heavy drinkers, and interferes with the distribution of oxygen and nutrients to the liver's cells. If the condition persists long enough, the liver cells will die, forming fibrous scar tissue (the second stage of liver deterioration, or fibrosis). Some liver cells can regenerate with good nutrition and abstinence, however in the last stage of deterioration, or cirrhosis, the damage to the liver cells is the least reversible.

Pancreatitis

The pancreas is a large gland located behind the stomach and next to the duodenum (the first section of the small intestine). The pancreas has two primary functions:

1. To secrete powerful digestive enzymes into the small intestine to aid the digestion of carbohydrates, proteins, and fat.
2. To release the hormones insulin and glucagon into the bloodstream. These hormones are involved in blood glucose metabolism, regulating how the body stores and uses food for energy.

Pancreatitis is a disease in which the pancreas becomes inflamed. Pancreatic damage occurs when the digestive enzymes are activated before they are secreted into the duodenum and begin attacking the pancreas.

There are two forms of pancreatitis: acute and chronic.

Acute pancreatitis is a sudden inflammation that occurs over a short period of time. In the majority of cases, acute pancreatitis is caused by gallstones or heavy alcohol use. Other causes include medications, infections, trauma, metabolic disorders, and surgery. In about 10% to 15% of people with acute pancreatitis, the cause is unknown.

The severity of acute pancreatitis may range from mild abdominal discomfort to a severe, life-threatening illness. However, the majority of people with acute pancreatitis (more than 80%) recover completely after receiving the appropriate treatment.

Chronic pancreatitis occurs most commonly after an episode of acute pancreatitis and is the result of ongoing inflammation of the pancreas.

In about 45% of people, chronic pancreatitis is caused by prolonged alcohol use. Other causes include gallstones, hereditary disorders of the pancreas, cystic fibrosis, high triglycerides, and certain medicines. Damage to the pancreas from excessive alcohol use may not cause symptoms for many years, but then the person may suddenly develop severe pancreatitis symptoms, including severe pain and loss of pancreatic function, resulting in digestion and blood sugar abnormalities.

Treatment for Pancreatitis

People with acute pancreatitis are primarily treated with intravenous fluids and pain medications in the hospital. In up to 20% of people, the pancreatitis can be severe and require admission to an intensive care unit (ICU). In the ICU, the person is closely monitored, since pancreatitis can cause damage to the heart, lungs, or kidneys. Some cases of severe pancreatitis can result in death of pancreatic tissue (pancreatic necrosis). In these cases, surgery may be necessary to remove the damaged tissue if a secondary infection develops.

Chronic pancreatitis can be somewhat difficult to treat. Doctors will try to relieve pain and improve the nutritional and metabolic problems that result from loss of pancreatic function. People are generally given pancreatic enzymes or insulin, if these substances are not being secreted or released by the pancreas. Pancreatic enzyme pills are usually prescribed to be taken with meals to aid in nutrient absorption. A low-fat diet may also be helpful.

Surgery may help relieve abdominal pain, restore drainage of pancreatic secretions, treat chronic pancreatitis caused by blockage of the pancreatic duct, or reduce the frequency of attacks.

People must stop drinking alcoholic beverages, follow their doctor and dietitian's dietary recommendations, and take the proper medications in order to have fewer and milder attacks of pancreatitis.

Esophageal Varices

Bleeding esophageal varices are enlarged veins in the walls of the lower part of the esophagus (the tube that connects the throat to the stomach) that bleed.

Scarring (cirrhosis) of the liver is the most common cause of esophageal varices. This scarring reduces blood flowing through the liver. As a result, more blood flows through the veins of the esophagus. This extra blood flow causes the veins in the esophagus to balloon outward. If these veins break open, they can bleed severely. Any type of chronic liver disease can cause esophageal varices.

People with chronic liver disease and esophageal varices may have no symptoms. If there is only a small amount of bleeding, the only symptom may be dark or black streaks in the stools.

If larger amounts of bleeding occur, symptoms may include:

- Black, tarry stools
- Bloody stools
- Light-headedness
- Paleness
- Symptoms of chronic liver disease
- Vomiting
- Vomiting blood

The goal of treatment is to stop acute bleeding as soon as possible, and treat varices with medicines and medical procedures. Bleeding must be controlled quickly to prevent shock and death. If massive bleeding occurs, the person may be placed on a ventilator to protect the airways and prevent blood from going down into the lungs.

Treating the causes of liver disease may prevent future bleeding. Preventive treatment of varices includes medications such as beta blockers or endoscopic banding. Bleeding often comes back without treatment.

Bleeding esophageal varices are a serious complication of liver disease and have a poor outcome. Liver transplantation may be considered for some patients.

Wet Brain

Wet brain is a form of brain damage. Wet brain is also called Wernicke-Korsakoff syndrome, Korsakoff's psychosis, and Wernicke's encephalopathy. The symptoms of wet brain sometimes improve with therapy but it is often permanent and irreversible.

Wet brain is caused by a deficiency of thiamine which is also known as vitamin B1. Alcohol consumption interferes with the absorption of thiamine. Wet brain has a sudden onset and is often brought on by a sudden large dose of glucose in an individual suffering from a severe thiamine deficiency. A sudden influx of glucose in a malnourished drinker can precipitate the onset of wet brain; therefore it is potentially dangerous for malnourished heavy drinkers to eat large amounts of sweets and no vitamins or other food.

It is generally agreed that wet brain occurs in two stages. The first stage of wet brain is Wernicke's encephalopathy, which results from a severe thiamine deficiency and which may be precipitated by a sudden influx of glucose. If Wernicke's encephalopathy is immediately treated with thiamine injections it can be reversed. If the Wernicke's encephalopathy goes untreated, it will progress to the second stage of wet brain, which is known as Korsakoff's psychosis, which is not reversible.

Anyone who drinks alcohol should always try to eat well and be careful to take vitamins. Very heavy drinkers may always feel too nauseous to eat much and they or their loved ones should at least try to make sure they get adequate vitamin supplements, particularly thiamine (B1). When malnourished heavy drinkers show up for medical treatment, doctors should be sure to give them vitamin shots or an IV with thiamine. Heavy drinkers need to be careful to get much more thiamine in their diets than non-drinkers because heavy drinking prevents much of the thiamine from being absorbed.

Symptoms of wet brain:

- Staggering, irregular gait, and poor muscle coordination
- Confabulation (remembering events that never happened)
- Inability to form new memories

- Loss of memory (this can be severe)
- Visual and auditory hallucinations
- Vision changes (including double vision, eyelid drooping, and abnormal eye movements)

Reverse Tolerance

In the average healthy human, alcohol is metabolized by the liver at the rate of about one standard drink per hour. People who frequently engage in heavy drinking develop tolerance, caused by changes in the brain and liver as these organs adapt to the steady presence of alcohol. When alcohol tolerance develops, people need to drink much more alcohol to get the same effect.

Reverse tolerance occurs when a heavy drinker develops liver damage and the liver no longer produces enough enzymes to break down alcohol. People with a lot of liver damage no longer metabolize alcohol well, resulting in intoxication on small quantities of alcohol. This phenomenon is known as reverse tolerance.

What is "Kindling"?

Some people who have repeatedly gone through "cold turkey" withdrawal without tapering off become more and more likely to have bad withdrawals from even small amounts of alcohol. This phenomenon is referred to as "kindling". People who have undergone kindling can suffer withdrawal seizures from drinking as little as a six-pack of beer.

Alcohol Poisoning and Alcohol Blackouts

Alcohol poisoning occurs when a large amount of alcohol is consumed, usually over a short period of time. The blood alcohol level is so high, it is considered toxic (poisonous). The person can become extremely confused, unresponsive, disoriented, have shallow breathing, pass out, or even go into a coma. Alcohol poisoning can be life-threatening and requires urgent medical treatment.

Alcohol blackouts generally occur when alcohol in the bloodstream spikes too high and too rapidly, exposing the brain to a sudden spike in blood alcohol content (BAC).

Some people have a much higher likelihood of experiencing alcoholic blackouts. These include people who have had gastric bypass surgery, people with long histories of severe alcohol abuse and withdrawal, and people with genetic irregularities in their alcohol metabolism.

Strategies to Prevent Blackouts

Eat – Eating a meal causes the valve between the stomach and the intestine to close for several hours, which greatly slows the influx of alcohol into the bloodstream and prevents BAC spikes.

Hydrate – Drinking a lot of water before consuming alcohol will reduce thirst helping one to drink more slowly and not spike the BAC.

Pace – Slow down drinking speed. One way to do this is to alternate non-alcoholic drinks with alcoholic drinks. Another technique is to time drinks with a watch.

Weaker Drinks – Avoid drinking straight shots of alcohol. As a general rule, the weaker the drink, the longer it will take to drink. Drinks that have taste often take longer to drink than tasteless ones. For example, most people will drink a gin martini more slowly than a vodka martini.

Rest – Many people have blackouts if they drink alcohol when they are sleep deprived. Being well rested before drinking will help avoid having blackouts.

Environment – Drinking in a strange environment can reduce tolerance to alcohol and increase the likelihood of blackouts.

Don't Mix Alcohol and Meds – Many medications can greatly increase the chance of blackouts if mixed with alcohol. Some are life-threatening. Medications that commonly lead to blackouts when mixed with alcohol include narcotic painkillers such as codeine, non-narcotic painkillers like aspirin, and nearly all sleep aids including antihistamines like Benadryl, and prescription sleep aids like Ambien.

Avoid Drinking Games – Drinking games or beer bongs can spike the BAC very quickly.

How to Taper Off Alcohol[50]

Going to a detox program and receiving medical supervision is recommended, because alcohol withdrawal can cause heart attacks and seizures. However, regardless of the risks, many people will not go to a detox center or seek medical intervention. It is less dangerous for someone experiencing withdrawal symptoms to know how to taper, than for the individual to quit "cold turkey".

DISCLAIMER: The information about how to taper off alcohol is for informational purposes only and is not a substitute for medical advice. It is safest to withdraw under medical supervision.

Some people can just quit drinking alcohol without having significant withdrawal symptoms. Other people, however, may suffer significant withdrawal symptoms when they suddenly stop drinking. Alcohol withdrawal is potentially fatal, so if experiencing significant alcohol withdrawal symptoms when stopping drinking, it is important to gradually detoxify from alcohol rather than quitting all at once. One can gradually detoxify by either by using alcohol itself or by using medications.

Who is likely to have significant alcohol withdrawal symptoms?

- People who have stayed intoxicated several days in a row
- People who have gotten intoxicated every night for a month or more
- People who have drunk small amounts throughout the day for a month or more
- People with a history of alcohol withdrawal symptoms

What Are Withdrawal Symptoms?

Withdrawal symptoms can be classified into three categories: mild, moderate, and severe.

- Mild or minor alcohol withdrawal usually occurs within 24 hours of the last drink and is characterized by tremulousness (shakes), insomnia, anxiety, panic, twitching, sweating, raised blood pressure and pulse, and stomach upset.

- Moderate or intermediate alcohol withdrawal usually occurs 24 to 36 hours after the cessation of alcohol intake. Its manifestations include intense anxiety, tremors, insomnia, seizures, hallucinations, high blood pressure, and racing pulse.

---

[50] Anderson, K. (2010) *How to Change Your Drinking* (Hamsnetwork.org).
- RICHARD D. BLONDELL, M.D., Ambulatory Detoxification of Patients with Alcohol Dependence. American Family Physician, Vol. 71/No. 3 (February 1, 2005) http://www.aafp.org/afp/20050201/495.html
- MAX BAYARD, M.D, et. al. Alcohol Withdrawal Syndrome. American Family Physician, March 15 2004. http://www.aafp.org/afp/20040315/1443.html

- Severe or major alcohol withdrawal known as delirium tremens (DTs) usually occurs more than 48 hours after a cessation or decrease in alcohol consumption. It is characterized by disorientation, agitation, hallucinations, tremulousness, racing heart, rapid breathing, fever, irregular heartbeat, blood pressure spikes, and intense sweating. When untreated, about one person in five will die of DTs. Some people refer to shakes as DTs, but this is inaccurate.

Even mild or moderate withdrawal can be dangerous for people with high blood pressure or weak hearts, because withdrawal raises blood pressure increasing the risk of heart attack or stroke. People with high blood pressure should seek medical consultation and need to taper.

A taper is needed if the following symptoms occur upon stopping:

- Hands are visibly shaky

- Excessive sweating

- Rapid or irregular pulse (a pulse of over 100 beats per minute is a danger sign)

How to taper?

People taper off by using alcohol or by getting prescription medications from their medical providers.

Beer is the best form of alcohol to use for or tapering. Attempts to taper off using wine or hard liquor are difficult because these have higher alcohol content than beer. Try to limit drinking to no more than necessary. Drink just enough to keep the sweats and shakes under control. Gradually reduce the consumption of beer as the taper continues. If the withdrawal is not too extreme, the taper should only take a day or two. Some tapers may take longer – three days or even a week. If symptoms of withdrawal persist, it is a sign that the taper is not done.

It is also very important when tapering, to prevent dehydration and to replenish lost vitamins. Medical detox may rehydrate with an IV and may also give vitamin shots. If doing a self-detox, be sure to drink lots of fluids and to take vitamins. Gatorade® is a good choice because it has balanced electrolytes.

Setting up a taper schedule:

It is very important to set up a taper schedule, which corresponds to the amount consumed and the amount of withdrawal one might have as a result. The first step in setting up a taper schedule is to estimate the daily baseline consumption of alcohol.

It is very important to estimate the baseline alcohol consumption in terms of standard drinks in order to set up a taper schedule. For reference: a standard (750-milliliter [ml]) bottle of wine at 12% alcohol contains 5 standard drinks. A 750-ml bottle of 80-proof alcohol contains 17 standard drinks. A liter of 80-proof alcohol is 23 standard drinks.

If drinking 20 or more standard drinks a day, then it is recommended that on the first day of the taper, drink one beer per hour starting in the morning for a total of 16 beers. On the second day, drink one beer every hour and a half for a total of ten beers. Then continue to taper down by reducing the amounts by two beers per day until down to zero.

If the baseline alcohol consumption is less than 20 drinks per day, reduce consumption by two standard drinks per day. For example, if drinking an average of 12 drinks per day then the taper schedule can be 10 beers the first day, 8 the second, 6 the third, 4 the fourth, 2 the fifth, and 0 the sixth day. Likewise, if the average consumption is 6 standard drinks per day, one can set a taper schedule of 4, 2, 0.

Some people choose to taper more quickly by cutting the amounts in half. For example, 20, 10, 5, 2, 0. But if you start having withdrawal symptoms, the taper is too fast and should slow down. Monitoring pulse and blood pressure is a very good idea while tapering.

Only people who are tapering down from very large quantities of alcohol such as a liter of vodka per day will need to start drinking in the morning in order to taper. If tapering from smaller quantities and feeling no withdrawal symptoms until afternoon or evening, then wait until the time the symptoms appear to begin to taper. Remember, drinking is not for pleasure; the alcohol is medicine, so only drink what is needed.

Taper using medications: Medical providers use benzodiazepine such as Valium or Librium. In some states, such as Minnesota, medical personnel are required by law to admit anyone suffering from alcohol withdrawal to an inpatient detox facility. In other states, the person may be allowed to attend an outpatient detox program or be given a prescription for benzodiazepines for self-detox.

Cross-Addiction and Cross-Tolerance[51]

The theory of cross-addiction states that if a person is addicted to one mood-altering substance, the individual is then addicted to all mood-altering substances, even ones he or she has never tried. This theory also states that the use of any mood-altering substance leads to relapse of the original substance.

Cross-addiction is not this clear-cut. Indeed, if one is addicted to an opiate like heroin, one automatically has cross-tolerance to other opiates like codeine or morphine. This is because all the opiates affect the same neurotransmitter system. However, a person who

---

[51] Anderson, K. (2010) *How to Change Your Drinking* (Hamsnetwork.org).

only uses opiates is not addicted to cocaine since cocaine affects a different neurotransmitter system. Likewise, someone who only uses cannabis is not addicted to alcohol, and so on.

Cross-tolerance is developing a tolerance to a drug and therefore having tolerance to closely related drugs. For example, Valium, Librium, Xanax, Ativan, and Klonopin are all closely related drugs, which belong to the benzodiazepine class of drugs. These drugs all affect the GABA receptors in the brain. Benzodiazepines can be substituted with each other because there is cross-tolerance. Alcohol also affects GABA receptors, explaining why benzodiazepines can be used to aid alcohol withdrawal. However, you cannot substitute heroin for Valium because heroin does not affect the GABA receptor. There is no cross-tolerance between heroin and Valium.

Heroin, morphine, codeine, methadone, etc. are all opiates and they all affect the brain's opioid receptors. If a person is addicted to heroin, that person can use another opiate such as codeine or methadone to prevent withdrawal because these drugs have cross-tolerance with each other.

Pharmacology for Addiction[52]

This is a summary of rapidly changing information. The use of medications should be supported when a person finds them helpful. Many people resist medications, and this needs to be respected. Clients have reported mixed responses to medications, but for some, they have been lifesaving.

Pharmacology for Alcohol Addiction

Naltrexone – Naltrexone blocks opioid receptors that are involved in the rewarding effects of drinking and the craving for alcohol. It reduces relapse to heavy drinking, defined as four or more drinks per day for women and five or more for men. Naltrexone cuts relapse risk during the first 3 months by about 36% but is less effective in helping patients maintain abstinence. Naltrexone can also be used for the treatment of opioids.

The Sinclair Method – As of April 2010, the most comprehensive reference on the Sinclair Method written for the public is *The Cure for Alcoholism* by Dr. Roy Eskapa, published in 2009. Until more sources become available, much of the information on the Sinclair Method comes from this source.

---

[52] National Institute of Drug Abuse (2009) *Principles of Effective Treatment: A Research Based Guide* (2nd edition) *Pharmacotherapies.*

The Sinclair Method treats alcohol use problems by combining medication with continued drinking. Someone following the Sinclair Method takes a 50-mg tablet of Naltrexone one hour before every drinking session. People who achieve success with the treatment experience a reduced urge to drink over time. The treatment is based on the theory called pharmacological extinction. It involves the use of competitive antagonists to endorphins being taken before alcohol consumption in order to block the endorphins from being used by the drinker's system. When the patient drinks without the endorphin reinforcement, it causes extinction. Use of this effect has been standardized into a technique called the "Sinclair Method", named after the man who first developed it, Dr. John David Sinclair.

The Sinclair Method has two steps: ingestion of an endorphin blocker followed by drinking. Naltrexone is the most commonly used endorphins blocker because Naltrexone is readily available and approved by the FDA for treatment of alcoholism. The Sinclair Method prescribes drinking "as you normally would" while taking Naltrexone.

The effects of the Sinclair Method can take from two weeks to several months before they become noticeable. This period increases if the person abstains from drinking, or largely drinks in an environment other than that in which he or she acquired the addiction. Taking Naltrexone without drinking will result in a small decrease in craving while the Naltrexone is being taken, but will not result in extinction.

The goal of the Sinclair Method is to return a person's desire for alcohol to the individual's rational control over a period of 3 to 15 months. The person may continue to drink because he or she perceives rational benefit to drinking, but will no longer be driven to drink by uncontrollable urges. Once the patient is no longer drinking on a daily basis, administration of Naltrexone is reduced to just those days during which drinking is expected, an hour before the drinking occurs. Taking Naltrexone before drinking will need to be done for the rest of the person's life; otherwise the endorphin conditioning will re-establish itself.

Acamprosate – Acamprosate (Campral®) acts on the GABA and glutamate neurotransmitter systems and is thought to reduce symptoms of protracted withdrawal, such as insomnia, anxiety, restlessness, and dysphoria. Acamprosate has been shown to help dependent drinkers maintain abstinence for several weeks to months, and it may be more effective in patients with severe dependence.

Disulfiram – Disulfiram (Antabuse®) interferes with degradation of alcohol, resulting in the accumulation of acetaldehyde, which, in turn, produces a very unpleasant reaction that includes flushing, nausea, and palpitations if the patient drinks alcohol. The utility and effectiveness of disulfiram are considered limited because compliance is generally poor. However, among patients who are highly motivated, disulfiram can be effective, and some patients use it episodically for high-risk situations, such as social occasions where alcohol is present. It can also be administered in a clinic or by a spouse, improving its efficacy.

Topiramate – Topiramate is thought to work by increasing inhibitory (GABA) neurotransmission and reducing stimulatory (glutamate) neurotransmission. At the time of this writing, its precise mechanism of action in treating alcohol addiction is not known, and it has not yet received FDA approval.

Pharmacology for Opioid Addiction

Methadone – Methadone is a synthetic opioid, used medically as an analgesic and a maintenance anti-addictive for use in patients with opioid dependency. It was developed in Germany in 1937. Although chemically unlike morphine or heroin, methadone acts on the same opioid receptors as these drugs, and thus has many of the same effects. Oral doses of methadone can stabilize patients by mitigating opioid withdrawal syndrome. Higher doses of methadone can block the euphoric effects of heroin, morphine, and similar drugs. As a result, properly dosed methadone patients can reduce or stop altogether their use of these substances.

Methadone maintenance treatment is usually conducted in specialized settings (e.g., methadone maintenance clinics). These specialized treatment programs offer the long-acting synthetic opioid medication, methadone, at a dosage sufficient to prevent opioid withdrawal, block the effects of illicit opioid use, and decrease opioid craving.

Suboxone and Subutex – Both of these drugs that have been approved by the FDA for the treatment of opiate addiction and contain the same active ingredient, Buprenorphine.

Buprenorphine – Buprenorphine is a semi-synthetic opioid that works as both an opiate and as an opiate blocker. Buprenorphine is a partial agonist (agonistic drugs are those that work to mimic the effect of a neurotransmitter in the brain) and has only a limited ability to activate opioid receptors. It can fill them up enough to stop someone from feeling sick, but it cannot activate these receptors enough to cause euphoria.

It reduces or eliminates withdrawal symptoms associated with opioid dependence but does not produce the euphoria and sedation caused by heroin or other opioids. It is administered in tablet form for placement under the tongue in 2- to 8-milligram doses. Patients taking this drug must be under a doctor's supervision and attend regular counseling sessions. It also has an analgesic, or pain-blocking effect.

Buprenorphine is considered "sticky", which means it will bump other drugs out of opioid receptors and "stick" on these opioid receptors very well. If taking Buprenorphine and heroin at the same time, the Buprenorphine would bump out all of the heroin and stick on the receptors, not allowing the heroin to have its normal effect.

As a partial agonist, Buprenorphine, even in high doses, is unlikely to slow breathing to a dangerous level. It is much harder to overdose on Buprenorphine than on normal "full agonist" opiates, such as heroin or methadone.

Subutex does not contain Naloxone. Suboxone does.

- Subutex contains a single active ingredient: Buprenorphine.
- Suboxone contains two active ingredients: Buprenorphine and Naloxone.

Suboxone contains a second medication, Naloxone, which is added to the formulation to keep people from abusing the medication. Due to this decreased risk of abuse and diversion, doctors have greater freedom to prescribe Suboxone in take-home doses (unlike methadone, for example, which is almost always distributed in single daily doses).

What Does Naloxone Do?

Naloxone works as an opiate antagonist (block receptors). It fills the opiate receptors in the brain and prevents other drugs from activating these receptors. But unlike Buprenorphine (which fills and activates receptors), Naloxone does not activate opiate receptors. With all receptors full but not activated, a person feels immediate and intense withdrawal pains.

When taking Suboxone as directed (letting the pill dissolve under the tongue), the small amount of Naloxone contained within has no noticeable effect. The Buprenorphine travels to the brain, providing relief from withdrawal symptoms.

If abusing Suboxone by injecting it, the Naloxone becomes fully activated resulting in a state of withdrawal. This state of withdrawal cannot be reversed by taking heroin or other opiate drugs.

Buprenorphine carries a low risk of overdose.

In 2000, Congress passed the Drug Addiction Treatment Act, allowing qualified physicians to prescribe Schedule III, IV, and V medications for the treatment of opioid addiction. This created a major paradigm shift that allowed access to opioid treatment in general medical settings, such as primary care offices, rather than limiting it to specialized treatment clinics.

Physicians who provide office-based Buprenorphine treatment for detoxification and/or maintenance treatment must have special accreditation. These physicians are also required to have the capacity to provide counseling to patients when indicated or, if they do not, to refer patients to those who do.

Patients stabilized on adequate, sustained dosages of methadone or Buprenorphine can function normally. They can hold jobs, avoid the crime and violence of the street culture, and reduce their exposure to HIV by stopping or decreasing injection drug use and drug-related, high-risk sexual behavior. Patients stabilized on these medications can also engage more readily in counseling and other behavioral interventions essential to recovery and rehabilitation.

Stimulant Addiction

An article posted in *Science Daily*[53] describes the potential for development of a first-ever pharmacological treatment for cocaine addiction.

A common beta blocker, Propranolol, currently used to treat people with hypertension and anxiety, has shown to be effective in preventing the brain from retrieving memories associated with cocaine use in animal-addiction models, according to Devin Mueller, University of Wisconsin – Milwaukee (UWM) assistant professor of psychology and a co-author with James Otis of the research.

This is the first time that a therapeutic treatment has been shown to block the retrieval of memories associated with drug addiction, a major reason many addicts experience relapse, says Mueller. The research is published in the August issue of the journal *Neuropsychopharmacology*.

Currently, "exposure therapy" is used to help recovering addicts suppress their drug-seeking behavior. In this therapy, the patient is repeatedly exposed to stimuli that provoke cravings but do not satisfy them. Done repeatedly over time, the patient experiences less craving when presented with those stimuli. The success of exposure therapy, however, is limited. Combining therapy with the use of Propranolol, says Mueller, would boost the effectiveness of the treatment.

Propranolol was chosen for the memory study because it has been used before to ease some withdrawal symptoms experienced by recovering cocaine addicts. Those using the drug were able to continue exposure therapy for longer periods than those without the

---

[53] *Science Daily* (July 18, 2011) New discoveries by researchers at the University of Wisconsin-Milwaukee (UWM) offer potential for development of a first-ever pharmacological treatment for cocaine addiction.

drug. In order to develop a drug treatment for overcoming relapse, the next step in the research is to determine where in the brain Propranolol acts to mediate the retrieval of cocaine-associated memories.

The study was funded by the National Institute on Drug Abuse, one of the National Institutes of Health, and by the UWM Research Growth Initiative.

According to Dr. Gabor Maté:

'There is no drug analogous to methadone to help with cocaine addiction. There have been some potentially encouraging trials with methylphenidate (Ritalin) and other stimulant preparations, and I have had some limited success in prescribing such medications to decrease people's reliance on cocaine and crystal meth. For a few patients, the difference has been dramatic. I would like to see long-acting stimulants investigated more vigorously, despite their addiction potential. It would be preferable to have people dependent on an oral stimulant in a controlled dose than smoked or injected cocaine or crystal meth."[54]

Amino Acid Therapy

A relatively new form of addiction treatment, called amino acid therapy, is becoming a common practice in the care of addictions. My clinical practice does not use supplements, so I cannot attest to its merits, but the logic seems sound. Amino acid therapy (often including intravenous [IV] supplements) is an increasingly common intervention provided in many residential treatment programs.

Amino acids are the building blocks of proteins. Without the proper levels of amino acids, we cannot survive, as proteins are responsible for the structure and the function of our cells.

Amino acid therapy may very well represent a breakthrough in the treatment for neurotransmitter imbalance.[55]

Michael Orian, lead medical staff of Ranch Creek Recovery, explains the rationale for using Amino Acid Therapy:

In the conventional management of diseases, such as depression and anxiety disorders, patients are often prescribed medications such as selective serotonin re-uptake inhibitors (SSRIs) (Celexa, Prozac, and Zoloft) or serotonin-norepinephrine reuptake inhibitors (SNRIs) (Effexor, Pristiq, and Cymbalta) to increase circulating levels of neurotransmitters.

---

[54] Maté, G. (2010) *In the Realm of Hungry Ghosts* (p 337).

[55] Bundrant, M. (2011) Amino acid therapy for depression, anxiety, ADHD, addiction and more. Natural News http://www.naturalnews.com/034030_amino_acids_addiction.html#ixzz23umCDNxG

By increasing the neurotransmitters, serotonin and norepinephrine, these medications are able to bind to receptors leading to changes in mental function and stabilization of many mood disorders.

There have been deficiencies in several neurotransmitters associated with attention deficit hyperactivity disorder (ADHD) including dopamine, norepinephrine, and acetylcholine. Once again, conventional treatment of this disorder often involves the administration of a medication that alters transport of these neurotransmitters within the brain such as Adderall and Strattera.

The use of pharmaceutical intervention can be successful in some patients; however, we are all individuals and may not all fit into the same box. Rather than changing the body's use of amino acids through altered transport, one alternative is to supplement amino acid precursors to neurotransmitters. While amino acid supplementation for the purpose of replenishing neurotransmitters has been a controversial topic in the medical community for many years now, in clinical practice, I have seen dramatic responses to oral amino acid supplementation for some of the above-mentioned diseases.

Typically, amino acids can be obtained through proper diet in a healthy individual. However, in the presence of disease, such as depression or addiction, it may be difficult to obtain proper amino acid levels through diet alone. Therefore, we may need to supplement amino acid precursors in a concentrated form to achieve proper circulating levels that can impact our health.

By supplementing precursor amino acids such as tryptophan, tyrosine, and glutamine, we are feeding our bodies with the building materials needed to make the neurotransmitters serotonin, dopamine, norepinephrine, and GABA, among others. For this conversion to take place, however, we also need coenzymes and cofactors such as vitamin C, folate, and S-Adenosyl Methionine (SAMe), which may be safely administered through an IV by a qualified health care professional.

In the context of addiction, particularly to drugs and alcohol, an individual may have severe imbalances in his or her neurotransmitter levels resulting in symptoms of depression, anxiety, insomnia, and jitteriness among others. This is often compounded by overt vitamin and mineral imbalances and poor absorption of nutrients through the intestines, causing problems in the body's innate ability to form neurotransmitters. By supplementing amino acids along with vitamins, minerals, and coenzymes, we can often reestablish proper levels of circulating neurotransmitters, thus minimizing or potentially eliminating side effects of withdrawal.

Studies and articles written by Dr. Kenneth Blum, frequently appear in response to searches for evidence of the proven effectiveness of using supplements. He markets a product called, SynaptaGenX, stating it represents the latest in amino acid therapy for addictions, and it is the result of more than 30 years of research and 23 clinical trials. It is a neuroadaptagen amino acid therapy utilizing a patented liposomal technology that improves absorption and maximizes bioavailability. The primary purpose of SynaptaGenX is to help regulate cravings. It also helps support focus and cognition, enhanced energy, neurotransmitter balance, optimal brain function, and healthy moods.[56]

The book, *Seven Weeks to Sobriety*, written by Joan Larson, details a self-treatment program designed to take someone from addiction to sobriety in just seven weeks. Her book is based on the treatment format developed at Health Recovery Center in Minneapolis. It concludes that psychological problems (mood swings, anxiety, and depression) are distortions of brain chemistry brought on by alcohol use or genetics; thus treatment involves stabilizing the brain at a molecular level by utilizing specific "biochemical repair". Her program claims a 74% success rate.

While amino acid and nutrition-based therapy sounds promising, some remain skeptical.

Posted on WebMD (June 2011) by Dr. Anthony Tornay, M.D. from the Betty Ford Center:

"Amino acids are building blocks for proteins, and nutritional therapies for disease have been an area of interest for centuries. Specific amino acids are needed to make certain brain neurotransmitters (dopamine, serotonin, etc.) and therefore are of interest in chemical dependency. While restoring adequate nutrition should be a focus in any person seeking treatment for addiction, there are no good controlled studies that show any benefit to specific nutritional supplements such as amino acids."

This chapter has included a lot of varying information about how environments, drugs of abuse, and medications can affect the brain. The following chapter helps integrate insights from neuroscience into specific program strategies and activities.

---

[56] http://www.nupathways.com/

Chapter Five

The Minnesota Alternative Model for Treatment

"We really need…and I know this is going to sound kind of corny…we need to be very loving, very accepting, and very patient with people who have these problems. And if we are, they will have a much higher probability of getting better." – a quote from Dr. Bruce Perry in his interview with Dr. Gabor Maté.

Decades of careful scientific research indicate that psychotherapy success is influenced by the client, the therapist, the treatment method, the context, the relationship between the therapist and the patient, and other factors. However, the therapy relationship accounts for why clients improve—or fail to improve—as much as the particular treatment method.[57]

Connecting with the people we serve is a predictor of their success.

This chapter provides a program overview, details about the treatment model, examples of treatment activities, information about the philosophy and culture and lastly, a description of ideal staff characteristics.

Program Overview

Minnesota Alternatives provides adult outpatient treatment for substance use disorders and consultation services that focus on engagement, skill development, personalized and holistic interventions, and concepts from neuroscience. The program uses many state-of-the-art interventions, including meditation and mindfulness, as well as best practices such as motivational enhancements and cognitive behavioral strategies.

Program elements can be incorporated into a treatment program, but can also be utilized in other services such as outreach, case management, peer support, or other recovery-oriented settings.

The program specializes in serving people who experience both substance use issues and mental health problems; and is enrolled with the Minnesota Department of Human Services as a provider of Co-Occurring Services. However, a mental illness diagnosis is not required for one to be eligible for services.

---

[57] SAMHSA: National Registry of Evidenced Based Program and Practices. http://www.nrepp.samhsa.gov/Norcross.aspx

The mission of Minnesota Alternatives is to provide an innovative, state-of-the art, treatment option for people and to assist other providers who want to offer alternative approaches.

The treatment model blends different techniques and strategies from a variety of theoretical approaches that include:

- **Person-centered approaches including psychiatric rehabilitation** that focus on client partnerships to develop critical skills and supports with an emphasis on functioning and understanding the environments clients are striving to live in. Cognitive behavioral interventions teach clients to reframe unproductive thoughts and understand their ability to decide what meaning they want to attach to circumstances. An emphasis on recovery reflects principles of empowerment, self-determination, and core values of compassion and hope.

- **Motivational strategies** prioritize engagement. Staff meet people "where they are at" (stage-specific interventions) with skillful use of empathy and individualized goal planning. Harm-reduction principles embrace the full range of harm-reducing goals including, but not limited to, abstinence. This means that small incremental positive changes are seen as steps in the right direction.

- **Concepts from neuroscience** educate clients about basic brain functioning and their capacity to undo negative or harmful patterns and create new neurological pathways based on positive change. Mindfulness and meditation help clients learn to calm themselves, become more self-aware, and use mental rehearsal to change behaviors. Mindfulness helps to engage higher thinking and quiet the reward circuitry. Drug and alcohol education provides current information about how using impacts the body and brain.

- **Holistic and emotion-based interventions** help clients to experience emotions, learn to let go, change behavior, build positive experiences, and heal. This includes trauma-informed care, guided meditations, individual therapy that includes EMDR (Eye Movement Desensitization and Reprocessing) and holistic activities to help with stress reduction, relaxation, and increased energy flow.

- **Cultural humility** rests upon a lifelong process of self-reflection and self-critique rather than knowing lists of beliefs and practices. This means maintaining a respectful attitude toward diverse points of view, developing a partnership with each client that allows for exploration of differences and a collaborative treatment process.[58]

---

[58] Tervalon, M., Murray-Garcia, J. (1998) *Journal of Health Care for the Poor and Underserved,* "Cultural humility versus cultural competence: A critical distinction in defining physician training outcomes in multi-cultural education"

The Process of Change

The capacity for change depends upon many factors. Psychiatric Rehabilitation teaches professionals to explore the barriers clients may be experiencing regarding change.

Common barriers to change include:

- **Motivation** – Is change necessary? What is the level of motivation? Are factors that are motivating change external (legally mandated) or can the client identify internal benefits for change?

- **Support** – Are there supports to assist with change? The ability to change correlates to the client's perceived level of support. Change is difficult if the client feels alone in the process.

- **Knowledge** – Does the client have the knowledge needed? An individual may have motivation to change, but does not know how or where to begin.

- **Resources** – Does the client have the needed resources? Motivation may be high, but may not be enough without adequate resources.

- **Skills** – Does the client have the skills? Despite a strong felt need, if people do not have the tools to bring about change, it probably will not happen.

Once these barriers are known, interventions can be tailored accordingly.

A popular belief is people need to "hit bottom" before they are ready to change. Yes, some people change because they are suffering or the consequences are severe. However, another important reason people change is that when they learn enough, they want to change.

The Minnesota Alternatives Treatment Model

Minnesota Alternatives strives to inspire people to change. This is accomplished by focusing on engagement, providing relevant information, and effective interventions. A client affirmed this by stating, "I have learned more useful information in the last 20 minutes than I have in all my other treatment experiences combined."

Assessment

Minnesota has very prescriptive requirements outlining what must be included in the assessment process based on the six ASAM (American Society of Addiction Medicine) dimensions. Clinicians assign a severity rating for each dimension including; intoxication/withdrawal potential, biological/medical conditions, emotional/cognitive issues, client acceptance/stage of change, relapse potential, and the recovery environment. For licensed addiction treatment providers, assessments must be completed within three treatment sessions. Programs that provide co-occurring services must screen for mental health issues, and if positive, conduct or obtain a diagnostic assessment completed by a qualified mental health professional.

Treatment requirements for co-occurring programs in Minnesota are currently under revision. Draft language calls for additional tools to screen for trauma, longitudinal/functional assessment, and standardized formats to determine the client's stage of change.

A common error made by both mental health and addiction providers is they risk losing clients by the early emphasis on paperwork, especially for clients who are ambivalent about seeking care in the first place. Many clients would have not returned if the first sessions were focused on formal assessment tools and screens. Clinicians need to be sensitive to where people are and put the primary focus on engagement. Take the time to talk casually and answer any questions or concerns about the treatment process. Create a dynamic where the individual is choosing you, as opposed to you choosing them. This lays the groundwork for person-centered care, trust, and client-staff partnerships. Yes, the paper work needs to get done, but pace it with engagement.

The following section organizes essential elements of treatment and service provision into three primary areas:

- Support/Counseling
- Education/Inspiration
- Accountability

As stated above, barriers to change vary from person to person. Some clients may have a great deal of knowledge but lack support or accountability. Others may have plenty of accountability, but lack support. The program offers a wide array of interventions and the clients and staff work in partnership to determine what the person needs, based on his or her unique situation.

Example: A woman enters treatment with a well-established mindfulness practice and a good understanding about neuroscience and how drugs and alcohol affect her body and brain. She lives alone, has a hard time following through on her goals, and experiences a great deal of loneliness. The focus of her treatment will rely less on educational interventions and more on support and accountability.

Support/Counseling

Interventions that focus on exploration, connection, engagement, healing, and support.

- **Motivational strategies** focus on engagement and meeting people "where they are at" (stage-specific interventions). People come to treatment because they find it helpful and enjoy themselves. An essential first step is addressing barriers to engagement.

- **Person-centered approach** fosters self-determination whereby clients identify what they want to work on and interventions that reflect the client's stated goals. They are motivated by what they define as important, instead of complying with goals defined by the program.

- **Client vision of recovery** is the first step in the treatment planning process. It promotes self-efficacy and hope. This is a written statement that identifies what would be happening in the client's life if "everything were going his or her way." The vision may or may not address substance use. Ask questions like: where will you be living, what will you be doing with your time, who is in your life, how will you be feeling?

- **Empathy skills** are a core element of all service provision. Clients are validated and heard. This promotes engagement, disclosure, and a sense of belonging. This is an essential skill required by all counseling staff, and a key element to Motivational Interviewing.

- **Understanding motives** seeks to clarify the primary motives for substance use and explore alternative ways these needs/motives can be met. The worksheet titled *Understanding Motives or Reasons for Use* helps with this exploration.

- **Evaluating the pros and cons of use** seeks to understand the client's perspective about the benefits, as well as the consequences, of his or her substance use. It explores the client's readiness for change, develops discrepancies and identifies intentions about future use or abstinence. The worksheet titled *Evaluating the Pros and Cons of Use* provides a helpful format.

- **Individual counseling/therapy** provides 1:1 time (which most clients prefer) for individual counseling, therapy, and goal review. Individual time is also provided for alternative therapies that include Reiki and acupressure. Emotion-based interventions include intentional meditations and counseling to help with experiencing emotions and learning to let go.

- **Addiction Medicine** provided by an on-site psychiatrist who specializes in treating co-occurring disorders.

- **EMDR** is a type of psychotherapy for treating post-traumatic stress disorder (PTSD). EMDR uses one's own rapid, rhythmic eye movements to dampen the power of emotionally charged memories of past traumatic events.

- **Common sense practical assistance** to assist with a variety of practical "real life" needs. It can be very difficult to focus on educational material if you don't have food or shelter.

- **Long-term support** is available after successful completion of treatment. Clients are welcome to return one time per week for the rest of their lives for long-term support. The program also includes a weekend peer-led support group that is led by program graduates.

Education/Inspiration

Subjects vary, but a primary focus is on brain functioning and brain opportunities to learn to "think greater than how we feel." Clients report they find the information very relevant and helpful, and they often demonstrate effective use of the skills.

- **Concepts from neuroscience** educate clients about basic brain functioning and their capacity to undo negative or harmful patterns in their brains. They also learn how to create new neurological pathways that are based on positive changes.

- **Mindfulness, meditation, and imagery** are core interventions to help clients learn to calm themselves, become more self-aware and learn mental rehearsal to change behaviors. Mindfulness helps to engage higher thinking and quiet the reward circuitry. The focus is on empowerment instead of powerlessness.

- **Education on drugs and alcohol** teaches how the brain and body are affected by substance use. Education is provided about how drugs/alcohol mimic naturally occurring chemicals and how these chemicals affect the brain/body in different ways. Cross-tolerance and withdrawal symptoms/risks are addressed. The worksheet titled *Understanding Negative Consequences* helps clients identify the problems drug/alcohol abuse has caused in their lives. It also directs them to conduct and share their own research about the risks of abuse.

- **Skill development** teaches skills that are relevant to improving the quality of life. The skills focus on attitude and perceptions as well as understanding the environments clients are striving to function in. Skills are taught through educational groups, role plays, guided meditations, mental rehearsals, sharing stories about skill utilization and/or missed opportunities. Cognitive behavioral interventions teach clients to reframe unproductive thoughts and understand their ability to decide what meaning they want to attach to circumstances (See Chapter Six, "The Key Skills").

- **Mental health education** addresses mental health symptoms and symptom management. Education may include materials from the *Seeking Safety* curriculum for PTSD and substance abuse. Staff members understand Dialectical Behavioral Therapy (DBT) so they can assist clients with integrating DBT skills into their recovery. Staff uses a variety of other materials for teaching.

- **Illness Management and Recovery (IMR)** provides easy-to-use client education material that covers a wide range of topics. Some of the program worksheets are modified from the IMR materials. IMR is a mental health evidenced-based practice and the tool kit can be ordered free from SAMHSA.

Accountability

If you monitor or measure something it usually changes. Accountability interventions provide a structure for measuring and monitoring.

- **Individualized goal planning** ensures clients have a very active role in deciding what goals to focus on in treatment. Treatment plans are written using client language and are reviewed and updated frequently as goals are met or modified. The treatment plan provides a key structure for accountability, follow-thorough, and a concrete measure of success. The treatment plan is a dynamic tool instead of a "one-size-fits-all" template. Goal completion is one of the primary indicators for successful completion of treatment. An example of an Individual Treatment Plan (ITP) is included in the Appendix.

- **Identifying harm/use reduction goals** is used when clients do not have abstinence as a goal. Although the majority of clients may have a goal of abstinence, some do not. Writing treatment goals that specify reduced use, or limited use of one substance while maintaining active use of another, is likely a departure from conventional practice. However, writing goals that are an accurate reflection of the client's intentions promotes honesty and supports partnership and self-efficacy.

- **Defining parameters** identifies the client's own set of parameters about his or her use and/or using behavior. This is for clients who intend to continue to use and is defined in partnership with the client. How much is too much? Examples may include: spending X amount of money, using heroin or meth, using more than X amount, etc. Parameters are essential so staff and the client know if and when the client's plan needs to be modified or the client may need other resources that may include a different level of care.

- **Substance use review** (see form) that outlines a process to review incidents of use. It explores motives for use, skill utilization (or lack thereof), and the possible need for changes to the treatment plan. This tool can be used for any use if someone has a goal of abstinence or when someone uses outside his or her defined parameters.

- **Self-monitoring and record keeping** of a behavior often changes it. Clients are more likely to change a behavior if someone is keeping track. Encourage clients to keep "use logs" and request to see them as part of their treatment planning and review.

- **Agreements** are useful tools for accountability. Short-term agreements can include a hand shake, good eye contact, or a written contract, and can be made with staff, with the group, with a peer or any combination thereof. Some clients do not have others to whom they are accountable. They find making agreements a useful tool to change a behavior or accomplish a goal. For an example, see the form titled *Personal Agreements*.

- **Managing high-risk situations** can be done throughout the treatment process. It identifies various high-risk situations and establishes plans and skills to manage them. As a client progresses through treatment, the risk factors often change. A well-developed plan is also part of discharge planning. See the form *Managing High Risk Situations*.

- **Engage relevant others** (family, natural supports) whenever possible. When permitted, engage them as part of the team to help with support and accountability. "Family" meetings are done with each individual family (instead of group education) to help ensure the unique needs of the family are addressed. For example, some family meetings may involve education, while others may address boundaries, self-care, communication, or limit setting.

Stage-Specific Treatment

Professionals have expressed concern that combining clients in groups that are in the early stages of change can be harmful to those that are in stages of action or maintenance. This has not been our experience. Besides, how would you split a client who may be in action stage on one issue, but pre-contemplative about a different issue?

It is important that prior to admission, potential clients are informed of the model of treatment including the principles of harm reduction. Some people are uncomfortable with this and choose to go elsewhere. Others may choose to try this approach and find it too difficult to be in treatment with clients who are actively using. This is validated and clients are assisted to find a program that better matches their needs.

An ideal service system allows for informed choice and ensures that people have options for care. Clinical experiences show that clients who choose abstinence do well in treatment with clients who are using if the program fosters a culture of acceptance and individualization. If the program genuinely accepts people "where they are at" and tailors the interventions accordingly, clients practice this same level of acceptance. Goals of abstinence are just as accepted as goals of non-problematic use.

Once in a while, a client will request to be put on a "zero tolerance" treatment plan, meaning the client wants his or her plan to reflect that no use will be tolerated, thus an external control is necessary.

Strategies for stage-specific programming include:

- Provide education groups regarding the stages of change and have group members identify which stage they are in. Remember clients may be in different stages for different substances. For example someone may be in action stage regarding cocaine use, but in pre-contemplation stage for use of alcohol.

- Provide open talk/check-in sessions that allow for clients to talk about whatever they want to (within reason of course). This provides a forum to learn from each other, get support, and share openly regardless of what stage a person is in.

- Have open discussions about the principles of harm reduction including the challenges, tensions, and opportunities this approach can create. Sharing experiences with others who are actively using mimics real life and teaches acceptance of others, refusal or limit setting opportunities, and shared insights.

- Share skill stories that include skillful behavior as well as missed opportunities. When teaching key life skills, structure the group by teaching first and then having clients share examples of when they effectively used the skills and/or missed chances including the results of these experiences.

- Have clients lead educational discussions, peer support groups, and activities. It fosters engagement, leadership, and peer-to-peer interactions. The clients typically have more knowledge about drugs and alcohol than the staff and staff can learn from the clients.

- Individual treatment planning and 1:1 counseling also provide opportunities to address each person's stage of treatment.

What happens if someone comes to treatment under the influence of drugs or alcohol?

The focus is on the person's behavior. The person will be asked to talk about his or her use and will be encouraged to not use prior to attending treatment in the future. There have been some circumstances when clients are actively working on a use-reduction plan that allows for use prior to attending, and this only occurs if safety issues are addressed. Staff can measure blood alcohol concentration (BAC) to determine if the person has been using alcohol. Clients who are over .08 BAC or who present as impaired will not be permitted to drive. People can be arrested for a Driving While Impaired charge even if under .08 BAC if there is evidence of alcohol use and the person's behavior is impaired. If reasonable, clients may be permitted to rest, eat, and remain on-site until their BAC has reduced to a legal level and they no longer present as impaired. Based on experience, clients are able to accept peers who are using providing their behavior is not disruptive.

Drug Testing/Urine Analysis (UAs)

UAs should only be used in an engagement, motivational interviewing manner to engage people. Since the program culture promotes honesty, the "we are going to catch you" dynamic is nonexistent. Clients are offered UAs if they feel it will provide an external motivation (i.e., to help provide an incentive to get through the weekend or to manage a high-risk situation). Some clients request UAs for their own peace of mind or for someone who may desire testing like a probation officer of family member.

UAs are useful tests that should only be used in a collaborative treatment plan, not as a police technique. Many programs use UAs in a way that is often detrimental to the therapeutic alliance, which is the most important predictor of positive outcome.

Criteria for Completion

Clients graduate when they have accomplished their treatment goals and when they feel ready to manage their issues without program support. Completion is not linked to the number of hours or days completed. Some clients come into treatment having already "done their work" but the courts are requiring they complete a treatment program so the length of their engagement is quite brief. Others have very complex needs and/or are in a very early stage of change and may need to attend for a year or longer. The frequency/intensity of the service matches the needs of the person instead of a "one size fits all" approach.

NIDA's principles of effective treatment highlight this point: [59]

Remaining in treatment for an adequate period of time is critical. The appropriate duration for an individual depends on the type and degree of his or her problems and needs. Research indicates that most individuals need at least 3 months in treatment to significantly reduce or stop their drug use and that the best outcomes occur with longer durations of treatment. Recovery from drug addiction is a long-term process and frequently requires multiple episodes of treatment. As with other illnesses, relapses to drug abuse can occur and should signal a need for treatment to be reinstated or adjusted. Because individuals often leave treatment prematurely, programs should include strategies to engage and keep people in treatment.

Successful completions are celebrated by providing a framed copy of a completion certificate, a peace token, and a song selected by staff that reflects the client's unique journey. At the graduation, everyone passes the token and shares wishes/observations. Family and friends are often included. A meal is then shared to complete the celebration.

Treatment Schedule

Minnesota Alternatives offers both day and evening hours. Day hours are available from 11am to 4pm (all sessions are mixed-gender but include breakout groups for men and women). The evening hours are Tuesday (men only), Wednesday (women only), and Thursday (mixed gender) from 5pm to 8pm. Clients put together a schedule that fits their needs. Often people choose to start with more hours and taper as they build other

---

[59] National Institute of Drug Abuse (2009) *Principles of Effective Treatment: A Research Based Guide* (2nd edition).

activities into their lives. Some clients may attend only once a week for a couple of hours while others may come 25 hours a week.

An example of the schedule:

Time:	Activity:
Day Program:	
11:00	Skills discussion
11:45	Group therapy/open talk
1:30	Lunch provided on site
2:00	Education
3:00	Meditation
3:30	Closure and integration activity

Evening Program:

5:00	Group therapy/open talk
6:30	Meditation
7:00	Education/skills discussion

The counseling staff meets weekly with clients for individual sessions that include counseling, therapy, goal review, practical assistance, and service coordination.

A holistic practitioner is on-site to provide Reiki and massage for relaxation, to promote healing, and offer stress relief.

The program is structured to also provide outpatient mental health services so a client can continue seeing the psychiatrist and/or therapist even after he or she has completed substance use treatment.

A registered nurse is available for consultation as needed.

Program Culture and Philosophy

Ideally, clients attend treatment because they find it welcoming, affirming, helpful, and a productive use of time. Engagement is a primary focus. Many treatment programs have a lot of rules, structure, rigidity, and clear ideas of right and wrong. Some examples of this include programs that discharge people for refusing to introduce themselves as addicts or alcoholics, or that require strict adherence to their schedule with little tolerance for tardiness or absences. I once interviewed a client who was seeking a program that would accommodate his work schedule and told him we could "piece together" a workable plan. He was so relieved because he had been told by another provider that "if he were serious about recovery, he would leave his job to get treatment."

Treatment should improve one's life, not interfere with life. A young man described a recent experience from another provider, "Nobody dared to speak up and challenge the staff or the program. People were afraid. One man did speak up, just before he was supposed to graduate, and he just disappeared."

People need to feel safe, and be given skills and opportunities to practice self-regulation/impulse control. Rigid, control-focused programs do not allow for this and may even do more harm than good.

The following **core principles** help to develop a culture that is authentic, useful, and client-centered:

- **Acceptance** – Allow clients to be open and candid about why they are attending and not judge or criticize their situation. For example, someone may be angry about being mandated to treatment: Validate their situation, and respond with, "It sounds like you are here to meet the requirements of probation, but since you have to be here, let's see if we can find something for you to do that is worth your time."

- **Flexibility/Tolerance** – Develop a schedule that fits client needs and other life obligations. Treatment is supposed to help with life, not get in the way of it. It is essential that the program hours and length of treatment are established based on each person's needs. Some people may attend a few hours per week for a few weeks, while others may come multiple times and for many months. The concept that everyone completes the same amount of treatment sessions makes no sense, as each person's needs are unique.

- **Honesty** – If the culture truly practices acceptance and meets people "where they are at", people will be honest. A client coined this phrase: Lying in the program is like lying on an eye test. It only means people will not get the help they need.

- **Generalizable** – Teach skills and educate about topics that directly relate to the day-to-day lives and cultures of the clients. This includes follow-up discussions about how the skills were used and missed opportunities for skill use.

- **Individualized** – Tailor program interventions and the initiation of services so they meet people "where they are at". People use substances for different reasons. It is important to understand the motives underlying substance use and then help people develop alternative ways to meet their needs.

- **Fun** – Laughter is good medicine and negates the toxic chemicals of stress.

Many people are mandated to attend treatment, and their focus is to "do what needs to be done" and get out of treatment as soon as possible. The following strategies help provide effective services regardless of the reasons people are attending:

Engagement Strategies

- Use Motivational Interviewing; clinician attitude and empathy skills are critical to engagement. Become proficient at rolling with resistance.

- Provide services that clients think are helpful. This will likely mean practical, hands-on help. Offer solution-focused help that addresses day-to-day needs.

- Reduce or eliminate barriers to attendance, such as transportation or hours of treatment.

- Have some flexibility with attendance and arrival times. The first activity of the day is more casual (skills talk or inspirational reading), which allows for late arrivals without being disruptive.

- Keep rules to a minimum. Avoid arguments/power struggles.

- Create a welcoming and warm atmosphere. Provide food and incentives for coming.

- Provide a quiet room with resting space that allows for solitude or rest. Anxiety is a common issue, and people need places for comfort and calm; this is not billable time.

- Teach relevant skills clients can practice at home that are easily incorporated into their lives.

- Provide a mix of activities that can be modified based on the client needs presented that day. For example, a theme of anger or boundaries may come up during the check-in session, so staff will modify the education activity to reflect these themes.

- Most people like guided meditations.

- Provide opportunities for clients to talk about whatever is on their minds (open talk groups).

- Provide peer support. Clients are useful teachers, coaches, and friends and have a lot of empathy and wisdom to offer each other. Clients may know best what they need to improve their lives.

- Find ways to laugh and have fun.

Staff Characteristics

One of most important factors in creating a culture that provides person-centered interventions and promotes a culture of honesty and openness is selecting the right staff and training staff members accordingly. Staff members serve as examples of the program skills and approaches.

The following characteristics are ideal staff qualities:

- **Ability to demonstrate mindfulness and regulate their emotions.** Staff members need to maintain a sense of calm regardless of what is happening.

- **Strong sense of compassion and desire to help others.** Program staff members are mission-driven and they genuinely care about people. They have chosen this field because of a desire to help.

- **Strong empathy skills.** This is a core element of all service provision. Clients are validated and heard. This promotes engagement, disclosure, and a sense of belonging. Staff members are skillful and willing to work with difficult stories and behavior.

- **Cultural competency.** Staff members recognize that a client's world view may differ from the mainstream, and staff helps each client work toward his or her own vision of recovery shaped by how the client views the world.

- **Good sense of humor and able to laugh easily.** While treatment can be intense and emotional, it can also be fun. Laughter is good medicine and it is important that everyone can laugh together.

- **A general sense of well-being and confidence so clients feel safe "unloading."** Staff members needs to practice basic self-care so they are well enough to provide care to others.

- **Ability to lead meditations and use imagery.** Meditation occurs each treatment session, so staff needs to be able to lead guided meditations and have experience with the practice.

- **Mental health knowledge and experience.** Strong mental health training and experience is essential. Many clients have co-occurring disorders and staff members need to know how to effectively respond. They need to understand various mental health issues including serious and persistent mental illnesses. Staff members need to understand and practice trauma-informed care.

- **Basic understanding about psychotropic medications.** Many clients take medications as part of their recovery from both substance use and mental health disorders. Staff members need a general understanding of different medications and when they may or may not be indicated.

- **Crisis intervention skills.** Staff members need to know how to handle an array of emergencies. This includes verbal de-escalation skills and knowing when emergency services may be needed. Staff members coordinate with other resources as necessary.

- **Ability to avoid power struggles.** It is essential that staff members understand the locus of control. Staff members can guide, teach, inspire, direct, counsel, but cannot ensure the safety of others. Staff members understand the scope of outpatient treatment and do not assume they can control the choices made by others. They are good at holding clients accountable for their own safety and they know how to avoid power struggles.

- **Flexibility and comfort with ambiguity.** Practicing harm reduction and individualized treatment means rolling with resistance and hanging in there with clients, even if they are making poor choices. Each client requires unique responses as no one size fits all. Staff members also need to be able to modify the daily treatment material based on the daily needs presented by the clients.

- **Willingness to think outside the box and take calculated risks.** Working with clients who are actively using drugs and/or alcohol requires the ability to tolerate risk and liability. Staff needs to be creative and engaging. It requires team work and consultation to know when parameters are exceeded. This includes when to refer clients elsewhere or discharge them for lack of progress.

- **Ability to use the program skills.** The skills are practical life skills and can be used regardless of whether someone has substance use or mental health issues. Staff members serve as examples of skillful behavior.

The staff helps clients develop an array of skills based on each person's needs. The following chapter details a list of "key skills" that are included in the treatment program. They provide practical life skills that anyone can use to improve their functioning and quality of their life.

Chapter Six

The Key Skills

The following key skills are a core part of the treatment process. They are easily integrated into the daily lives of clients. Clients (and staff) have consistently reported they find the skills useful and describe them as tangible additions to their tool box.

To review, skill development is part of the education "pillar" of treatment (the others being support/counseling and accountability). A skill is taught and/or reinforced during each treatment session. Staff (and clients) teach a skill and then share examples of skillful behavior or missed opportunities. For example: A client shares that he or she reframed some bad news (effective skill use), while another shares that he or she blew up at a partner (missed opportunity). The skill descriptions that follow are used to guide group discussions and can be used in individual sessions, or given to clients for homework/journaling exercises.

The key skills are listed below followed by a Sample Skills Grid. Following the grid, each skill is explained in greater detail with a separate "handout" that can be duplicated for skills training activities.

The grid provides a tool for self-evaluation of skill acquisition. Clients record the date and then self-rate how they are doing with mastery of each skill. Many clients report feeling proud of their progress when they see their skill ratings improve. Staff also demonstrate skill use. A staff member who was really struggling with her child said, "I just need to remember, nothing is permanent."

The Key Skills

- **Practicing Basic Self Care** – Eat, sleep, exercise, drink water and go outside to be with nature. I am less vulnerable if I am rested and fed. Quit polluting my brain and my body.

- **Calming Self through Breathing and Mindfulness** – Slow down and breathe deeply. Do not act. Allow the impulse to pass. Be mindful by noticing what is around me and try to be present in the moment.

- **Creating an Optimal Environment** – Everyone needs safety, connection with others, privacy, and order. Pay attention to my environment and who I surround myself with. Understand boundaries.

- **Experiencing Emotions** – Allow myself to experience difficult emotions by naming them, noticing how they feel in my body, stepping away from the story, and waiting for the sensations in my body to fade away. Ride the wave of the emotion.

- **Building Positive Experiences** – Create new neural networks based on positive memories, positive experiences, and positive emotions. Use imagery/visualization. Laughter neutralizes the negative effects of stress.

- **Cultivating Hope and Gratitude** – Choose to be hopeful, take time to notice all I am doing well and focus on my strengths and blessings. Learn to let go and practice forgiveness if I am holding onto resentments/anger.

- **Reframing** – Use my executive brain functions to decide the meaning I want to attach to circumstances. Learn to watch my thoughts and interrupt negative thought patterns. Meditation helps me train my mind and learn to focus.

- **Practicing Acceptance** – Refusing to accept situations I am unable to change only adds to my suffering. It is what it is.

- **Understanding Impermanence** – Remind myself that nothing is constant and these hard times will pass. Things will get better.

- **Practicing Attached Detachment** – Do my very best in life and then let go of the outcomes. Keep things in perspective.

- **Focusing on Effectiveness** – Pay attention to the goal I desire, and if needed, put aside pride or stubbornness and do what works. Be effective.

- **Demonstrating Understanding** – People are more likely to listen to me if I first demonstrate that I hear them.

- **Developing Meaningful Activity** – Find something to do that gives my life meaning and purpose.

Below is Sample Skills Grid for client self-rating using a plus, minus, or plus-minus. A numeric system could also be used. In the example below, the client has self-rated their perception of which skills are strengths (+), which skills are used but not as often as needed (+/-) and which are deficits (-).

A one-page Skills List and blank skills grid can be found in the appendix.

Skill Name	Date: 7/4/12	Date:	Date:	Date:	Date:	Date:	Date:	Date:
Practicing Basic Self Care	+/_							
Calming Self through Breathing and Mindfulness	+/_							
Creating an Optimal Environment	+/_							
Experiencing Emotions	_							
Building Positive Experiences	+							
Cultivating Hope and Gratitude	+							
Reframing	+/_							
Practicing Acceptance	+							
Understanding Impermanence	_							
Practicing Attached Detachment	+/_							
Focusing on Effectiveness	_							
Demonstrating Understanding	_							
Developing Meaningful Activity	+							

The remainder of this chapter includes handouts that detail each skill and can be used in groups, one-on-one, or for client homework/journaling.

Skill: Practicing Basic Self Care

Eat, sleep, exercise, drink water and go outside to be with nature. I am less vulnerable if I am rested and fed. Quit polluting my brain and my body.

Education: While this skill may seem obvious and simple, it is often overlooked and is essential as a building block for all the other skills. If we are not tending to our most basic needs, it can be difficult to control our emotions and more difficult to manage stressful events. We are at greater risk of engaging in bad habits. We are more prone toward irritability, low energy, and trouble just managing day-to-day life. Our memory is affected (shrunken hippocampus) by lack of sleep or excessive amounts of stress.

Here are some suggestions for basic self-care:

- Drink water, limit toxic substances, and eat balanced meals. Sugar is hard on our immune system. Try to eat whole (instead of processed) foods.

- Get enough sleep. Have strategies for sleep hygiene if needed.

- Have fun and tap into the powerful medicine of laughter.

- Engage in exercise we enjoy and can afford. Go for a walk.

- Get outside. See a tree, visit a river, and notice the flowers. Try growing something. Spending time in nature can promote mindfulness and calm. Sunshine provides Vitamin D, which is essential for good health.

- Limit time interfacing with technology. Be with live people, not virtual ones. We are hard-wired to connect with others.

- Find friends that offer as much as they take. Evaluate relationships and avoid having too many relationships where the balance of give and take is off.

- Be able to say no. Be intelligently selfish. Our capacity to give to others changes depending upon how resourced we are. Pay attention to how stretched we are and say no if needing to conserve resources.

- Find a support person who is a good listener or at least someone who is willing to learn how to listen. (See skill titled Demonstrating Understanding.)

- Manage stress. Learn how to use breathing as a method to calm down.

- Try new things. Get out of the box. Put on a favorite song and dance when no one is watching.

Questions for discussion and reflection:

- How much sleep am I getting? Recommendations are at least 7 to 8 hour or 4 cycles of REM.

- What am I eating? Can I find ways to eat more whole foods?

- How much water am I drinking? What does it mean to be dehydrated?

- Caffeine and alcohol are diuretics. What does this mean?

- How much do I smoke? Can I cut down? What resources are available to me?

- Have I been outside lately? What is nature deficit disorder? When was the last time I watched a sunset or looked at the stars?

- Am I getting any exercise?

- What can I do to practice better self-care?

- What types of relationships am I in?

- Are my friendships balanced?

- How often do I laugh?

- How much time am I in front of a screen or on my phone?

- When was the last time I had a physical?

- Am I getting enough Vitamin D? Should I have this tested?

Skill: Calming Self through Breathing and Mindfulness

Slow down and breathe deeply. Do not act. Allow the impulse to pass. Be mindful by noticing what is around us and try to be present in the moment (get out of our head).

Education: Learn how to breathe into the base of our lungs pushing the diaphragm down. Deep breathing is one of the easiest ways to improve the quality of our lives. The average adult uses only one-third of their lung capacity. Chronic tension and poor posture also contribute to poor breathing and thus poor health. Many people are "chest breathers", meaning they breathe from the chest and breathing is irregular and air intake is shallow. Diaphragmatic breathing is much healthier. It allows us to take in more air and to breathe it in more deeply.

Here is a picture of the diaphragm. The goal is to bring air deep into the lungs pushing the diaphragm down, and causing the abdominal area to expand when the breath comes in.

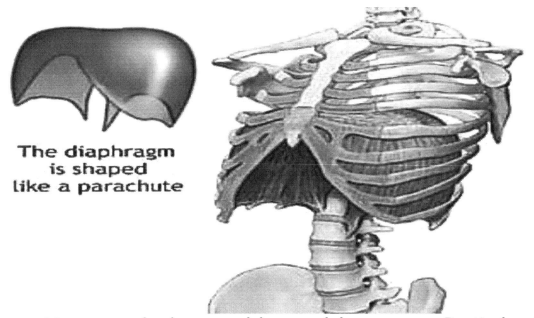

The diaphragm
is shaped
like a parachute

When practicing, put your hands on your abdomen and close your eyes. Practice breathing in and see if you can make your abdominal area expand.

What are the benefits of deep versus shallow breathing?

- **Triggers the Relaxation Response** – Diaphragmatic breathing activates the parasympathetic wing of the nervous system, and is a great tool for releasing tension from the body. It also reduces stress hormones in the body.

- **Boosts Energy and Increases Vitality** – Breathing deeply increases our energy levels as it allows fresh oxygen and nutrients to be more easily distributed to all the cells of our body. This helps the brain and all of the organs to function optimally.

- **Strengthens the Immune System** – Abdominal breathing helps prevent infection of the lungs and other tissues.

- **Improves the Circulatory System** – Diaphragmatic breathing benefits the circulatory system by increasing blood circulation and helping blood return to the heart.

- **Helps digestion** by massaging the internal organs as the diaphragm moves up and down.

When able to do diaphragmatic breathing, add the practice of mindfulness. This means being fully in the moment and not getting caught up in our thoughts.

Look at an item of interest (e.g., a flower, shell, colorful rock, painting) and really look at it while breathing diaphragmatically. "Notice that you notice" each and every detail, again not getting caught up in your mind. Simply breathe and notice. Practice mindful eating. Take a bite of something and take the time to chew it slowly, noticing the texture and the taste.

What are the benefits of mindfulness? Mindfulness raises self-awareness because we are fully in the present and able to observe. Being self-aware is the first step in creating positive changes in our lives. We need to notice what we are doing before we can change it. Mindfulness gives us the ability to slow down and pay attention to our thoughts, feelings, and behaviors. Mindfulness helps engage the control centers of the brain (frontal lobe) enabling self-regulation vs. impulsive or emotion-based/reward-driven reactions.

Supports for Mindfulness

- Slow down. Simplify our lives.

- Talk less.

- Do one thing at a time.

- Focus on our breath during daily activities.

- Relax into a feeling of calm presence with other people.

- Use routine events as "temple bells" to return us to center. For example, use the time driving to work to notice our breathing and "really see" what is before us.

- At meals, take a moment to reflect where our food comes from and eat with awareness of chewing and taste. Try to just eat, instead of multi-tasking during the meal.

- Notice that you notice. Then notice that you noticed that you noticed ☺.

Questions for discussion and reflection:

- How mindful am I? Am I aware of my thoughts and do I ever notice them and then decide to think differently?

- How impulsive am I? Do I often act without thinking?

- Do I ever breathe to calm or slow myself down? How can I remind myself to breathe deeply?

- Do I feel in control of my feelings or do I feel like they control me?

- When can I practice mindfulness?

Skill: Creating an Optimal Environment

Everyone needs safety, connection with others, privacy, and order. Pay attention to my environment and who I surround myself with. Understand interpersonal boundaries.

Education: Brains develop and function according to the environment that they develop and function in. It can be very easy to escape into substance use if our most basic needs of safety, security, privacy, and connectedness are not addressed.

How we feel is greatly determined by our living environments. A house full of clutter contributes to feeling overwhelmed or out-of-control, while a home that is organized and clean can help us feel in control and less stressed. Try to have at least one place in our home where we feel a sense of calm, safety, order, and control.

If feeling overwhelmed by a messy home, start with very small steps and just do a little bit at a time. The best way to manage overwhelming feelings is to take small steps. Remember, books are written one sentence at a time.

Personal boundaries can be very difficult to maintain or regulate. It is important to understand that our boundaries can be too rigid or too loose, and that boundaries should change based on different circumstances. For example, our capacity to "give" in relationships changes depending upon our well-being or our stress levels. Sometimes we can take on a lot, while other times we may need to reserve energy for our own well-being. Some people just give and give, even when they are not well themselves. Co-dependency is when we get so involved in someone else's problems that we start to suffer as a result.

The other extreme is living isolated lives that involve loneliness, boredom, and little sense of belonging to a greater community. Neurobiologists are now learning that loneliness has a profound effect on brain structure and functioning. Human beings are troop primates by nature. When we are faced with prolonged loneliness, it goes against our primal impulses to be a part of a group. We are hard-wired to connect with others.

Do what we can to create an optimal environment for ourselves. This includes both our physical surroundings as well as the people we choose to have in our life. Find ways to "play up". This means try to connect with others who have something to offer, people who we respect, who can mentor us, and who we can learn from.

Questions for discussion and reflection:

- What is my environment like?

- What needs to be done to make it more optimal?

- Do I feel safe and secure?

- Are my basic needs provided for?

- Is my home chaotic and cluttered?

- Do I have too much alone time, or not enough?

- Am I lonely? What prevents me from connecting with others?

- What steps can I take to be more connected with others?

- What types of boundaries do I have? Are they too loose or too rigid? Do I need to make different choices?

- Have I gotten overly involved in others' problems? How do I know if I am overly involved?

- Who is in my inner circle? Are they people that give as often as they take?

- Do I have any mentors or teachers in my life?

Skill: Experiencing Emotions

Allow myself to experience difficult emotions by naming them, noticing how they feel in my body, stepping away from the story, and waiting for the sensations in my body to fade away. Ride the wave.

Education: Before working on this skill, practice diaphragmatic breathing and mindfulness to ensure the ability to calm yourself. Use this skill in a safe place and/or in the company of someone trustworthy.

Slowing down and focusing on our breathing while experiencing emotions can help us relax into what we are feeling. Relaxation helps ease tension so we can try to name and describe our feelings.

Naming or describing feelings as sensations can help demystify them, making them less vague, frightening, uncomfortable, or overwhelming.

When we understand why we feel nervous, annoyed, hassled, driven, blue, etc., these feelings have less power over us. When using this skill, some people prefer to "step away" from the story, instead focusing all their attention on their breathing and what they are feeling in their bodies.

Trust that we can handle difficult feelings. People tend to give difficult feelings a lot of power which often results in being "feeling avoidant" and/or feeling like they are "on the run" from their feelings. Some people find that the primary reason they use mood-altering substances is to avoid difficult feelings.

Experience emotions as body sensations. Consider them as waves of sensation that peak and then subside. Let go of the story line, focus on your breathing, stay with the experience, trusting it will pass. Learning to feel emotions in your body allows you to step away from them.

A practice exercise:

1. Sit up straight, put your feet flat on the floor, roll around your neck and shoulders, and try to work out any tension you may be feeling in your body.
2. Take a deep breath into the base of your lungs. Feel your diaphragm push down causing your stomach to expand as you breathe in. Continue to breathe deeply, again bringing air into the base of your lungs, stomach expanding as the breath comes in.
3. Focus on your breathing...your mind starts to quiet.

4. Start by naming a painful or negative emotion that is holding you back. Give it a name and speak the name of the emotion in your mind.

5. Breathe.

6. As you name the emotion, feel it in your body. How does it feel? Where in your body do you feel it? Feel all the sensations that you can. Name the sensations... notice the feeling as it rises like a wave...and breathe.

7. While breathing, step away from the story. Allow the sensations in your body to exist.

8. Stay with the sensations until you feel them start to subside or mellow.

9. Continue to sit quietly. When the emotion lets up, take a couple of deep breaths, slowly open your eyes, and come on back.

Our capacity to sit with feelings increases as we practice, like strengthening a muscle. Once we know we can experience difficult emotions without them consuming us, or without resulting in self-harm, we understand the role emotions have in our life.

From the book *Tuesdays with Morrie*:

"If you hold back on the emotions—if you don't allow yourself to go all the way through them—you can never get to being detached, you're too busy being afraid. You're afraid of the pain, you're afraid of the grief. You're afraid of the vulnerability that loving entails."

Questions for discussion and reflection:

- Practice sitting with an emotion, either positive or negative.
- How did it go?
- What were you feeling in your body?
- How long did it take for the sensations to mellow?
- Was it helpful to step away from the story?
- What is your "relationship" with difficult feelings?
- Try marrying a painful feeling with a positive memory or affirmation.

Skill: Building Positive Experiences

Create new neural networks based on positive experiences, positive memory, and positive emotions. Use imagery/visualization. Laughter neutralizes the negative effects of stress.

Education: Positive experiences create new neural networks. Positive thoughts and actions counteract existing negative networks. Create more positive experiences to help ourselves build confidence and strength. Practice mentally rehearsing these activities over and over and we will feel more prepared to take emotional risks and action steps to improve our lives.

Laughter (even if induced) reduces the effects of toxic stress hormones in ways that none of our medications can replicate. Check into "Laughing Yoga" and learn ways to improve well-being through laughter.

When we have positive feelings and experiences, take the time to digest and sustain these positive states; let them wash over us. Wallow in times of happiness and joy instead of wallowing in times of remorse or pity. These positive memories and feelings can be recalled at other times and reproduce these positive effects.

- Functional MRI has led to dramatic increase in knowledge about the brain and the mind and we now know that what flows through our mind sculpts our brain.

- Deliberately "wallowing" in feelings of happiness will increase dopamine levels. Small positive actions every day change neural structure and add up to large changes over time.

- Science shows that if we train the brain to function in a positive state (instead of a stressed, neutral, or negative state) it becomes 31% more productive.[60]

Another approach to helping resolve difficult feelings is to "marry" them with a positive thought. According to *The Practical Neuroscience of Buddha's Brain*[61], painful experiences are often best healed by positive ones. When two things are held in mind at the same time, they start to connect with each other on a neurological basis.

An example of this is a former client who had a well-established brain and behavior pattern of despair and self-hate that led to binge drinking and monthly hospitalizations for many years. He learned to train his brain to use vivid imagery of one of his fondest memories from his childhood (fishing on the open water in a boat with his father) whenever he caught himself heading down the well-worn path of despair. He became skillfully self-aware and would interrupt his negative thought patterns with his favorite memory. He found this exercise very effective and successfully quit binge drinking and no longer needed hospitalization.

Questions for discussion and reflection:
- Can we train ourselves to watch our thoughts and then create new neurological pathways built on new ways of thinking?

- How much of my time is spent on negative thoughts?

- How much is spent on positive thoughts?

- What are some positive thoughts I can cultivate?

- What is my favorite memory?

- How often do I laugh? Practice laughing. Tell jokes or funny stories, practice belly laughing. Pretend you are Santa.

- What are some of my favorite things to do that bring me joy?

---

[60] Achor, S. (2010) *The Happiness Advantage: The Seven Principles of Positive Psychology That Fuel Success and Performance at Work.*

[61] Hanson, R., Mendius, R. (2009) *The Practical Neuroscience of Buddha's Brain.*

Skill: Cultivating Hope and Gratitude

Choose to be hopeful, take time to notice all I am doing well, focus on my strengths and my blessings. Learn to let go and practice forgiveness if I am holding onto resentments/anger.

Education: "A grateful heart is a healthy heart". People who express gratitude on a regular basis have better physical health, optimism, progress toward goals, well-being, and help others more.[62]

Gratitude and appreciation for the blessings (no matter how small) we have in our lives is a very important skill. Many cultures believe that we reap what we sow and/or that we get what we give. Taking a break from a problem-focused perspective and tuning in on appreciation and gratitude helps to develop traits of humility and graciousness.

Another word for hope is optimism, or choosing to see the bright side of things, choosing to see the cup as "half full" instead of "half empty", "making lemonade out of lemons", "finding the silver lining in every cloud."

Optimism can protect people from mental and physical illness. People who are optimistic or focus on happiness have better performance in work, school, and sports. They are less depressed, have fewer physical health problems and have better relationships with other people. Further, optimism can be measured and it can be learned.[63]

What resentments are we holding on to? Are there things from our past that we refuse to let go? Holding onto to resentments and anger can keep us from living life fully or to our greatest potential. Mind is matter. When we think negative or hurtful thoughts we also stimulate stress chemicals that contribute to poor health and greater risk for illness. Learning to forgive and let go does not mean we are approving or condoning the behavior. It means we are choosing to free ourselves from the negative and toxic effects that these feelings can create. We cannot simultaneously feel resentment and joy or anger and love.

Following are excerpts from an article in the local paper of a moving story about forgiveness:[64]

"Sally Packard had waited seven months to get the chance to talk to the teenager who stole her car, and with it some of her independence. The car, a 1989 Dodge, wasn't worth much. But it was important to Packard, age 76."

---

[62] Peterson, C (2006) *A Primer in Positive Psychology*, New York, NY: Oxford University Press.

[63] Seligman, M. E. P. (2002) *Authentic Happiness: Using the New Positive Psychology to Realize Your Potential for Lasting Fulfillment.*

[64] Tevlin, J. (March 17, 2012) *Star Tribune*, "Forgiveness, hope wins out over crime in juvenile court".

"When Packard finally got to meet the boy, 17, in Hennepin County Juvenile Court recently, she started with a quote:"

"'When we forgive, we don't deny the hurt that we have received. We don't deny that it was wrong, but we acknowledge that there is more to the offender than the offense.'"

"Then Packard talked about being a foster mom for about 50 kids, many of them who had been abused and neglected, and how much she empathized with the young man standing before her in court."

"'I personally know most of these kids have not been parented, and maybe their parents haven't either, or maybe they got into the wrong crowd, or got into drugs,' she said."

"Packard then asked the judge if she could give the young man two stones. One said 'Hope' the other said, 'A special prayer for you'."

"The young man took the stones, and began to sob."

"'The hurt, I never thought of that,' said the teen. 'I'm really sorry. I regret this decision. I'm sorry for all of the hurt that I caused you.'"

"'I care. Lots of people care about you!' said Packard."

"Then Packard did something none of the people in the courtroom had seen before. She hugged the person who had upset her life. He squeezed her hard and sobbed."

"By now, everyone in the courtroom was crying."

A quote by Jack Kornfield:

"At the end of life, our questions are very simple: Did I live fully? Did I love well?"

Questions for discussion and reflection:

- Define optimism and pessimism. Which am I? How can I become more optimistic?
- What are qualities I like in others? How can I cultivate these qualities?
- What do I have in my life that I am grateful for?
- How can I take time each day to give thanks for what I have?
- How does my life compare to others? Look at what is going on in other parts of the world to find blessings.
- Create a card or simple gift and give it to someone you appreciate.

- What resentments am I holding on to? Are there things from my past that I refuse to let go of?

- What would it mean to let go of these resentments?

- How are they helping me? How are they hurting me?

- What steps can I take to start to let go? Do I need to talk to someone, write a letter, or have some type of ceremony or ritual?

- Discuss the meaning of Jack Kornfield's quote.

Skill: Reframing

Use my executive brain functions to decide the meaning I want to attach to circumstances. Learn to watch my thoughts and interrupt negative thought patterns. Meditation helps me train my mind and learn to focus.

Education:

The skill of reframing can be described as a cognitive behavioral strategy. It is based on the idea that our thoughts, not external things (like people, situations, or events) cause our feelings and behaviors. This means we can change the way we think/feel and we can act or respond differently even if the situation does not change.

All of us continually decide what meaning we choose to attach to a set of circumstances or experiences. For example, we all are sitting here is this room together and having a discussion. If each of us were to write down what this experience means to us, we would likely all write down different thoughts.

A quote from Viktor E. Frankl in his book, *Man's Search for Meaning,* summarizes this point very well. Frankl, chronicling his experiences as a concentration camp inmate, concludes that a prisoner's psychological reactions are not solely the result of the conditions of his life, but also from the freedom of choice he always has even in severe suffering.

"The one thing you can't take away from me is the way I choose to respond to what you do to me. The last of one's freedoms is to choose one's attitude in any given circumstance."

Remember that humans have big brains that allow us to think greater than how we feel. Our frontal lobe is the "CEO" of the brain and regulates other parts of the brain. The reason this is important to understand is that even when faced with very difficult and painful circumstances, we can decide how we are going to respond.

This is easier said than done, and becoming skillful at mindfulness and diaphragmatic breathing will help us slow down so we can "think" things out. Learning how to meditate will also help us train our mind so we are less prone to acting from our emotion-driven midbrain. Using the skills of building positive experiences and cultivating hope and gratitude also trains our mind to continually reframe how we perceive things.

People who are skillful at reframing are often described as optimists and are generally well liked. They have the capacity to find silver linings, or opportunities in hardship.

The opposite is someone who is always negative and sees everything as a personal injustice or tends to see him or herself as a victim. As we know from experience, these are people that can be difficult to spend time with.

Questions for discussion and reflection:

- We all have our moments and tough times, but what can we do to reframe our personality toward the positive?
- Share an example of when you practiced reframing.
- Practice this skill by doing something as a group and share the different meanings experienced.
- When are other times I could use this skill?
- Read the quote by Victor Frankl and discuss what it means.
- Do I tend to react more from my emotion mind (midbrain) or my frontal lobe?
- Have I been using breathing and mindfulness to slow down and calm myself?
- What are some of my automatic thoughts and how can I reframe them?

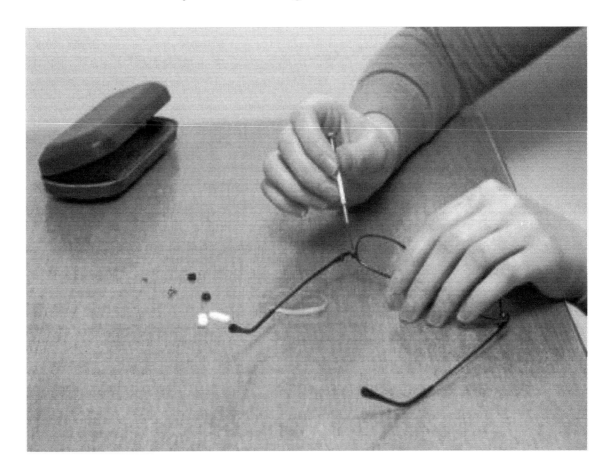

Skill: Practicing Acceptance

Refusing to accept situations I am unable to change only adds to my suffering. It is what it is.

Education: The key to understanding the use of this skill is the phrase, "situations I am unable to change". This skill is not an excuse to be complacent or disengaged. The point is to be aware of when we get upset about situations that cannot be changed.   A common example of this is getting stuck in traffic, or having to wait in a long line. More difficult examples are losing a loved one, an injury, or illness.

We want to know why something happened because we were hurt in some way, and if we can assign a reason "why" to the event, then we feel we can control the event in the future to keep it from happening again. It scares us to think that there are things in our world that we can't control. So we continue to analyze and search for the answer to "why did this happen." We look to the point of exhaustion because we don't want to experience that pain ever again.

There are numerous and frequent situations that we will never know the reason they happened. They just did. They are seemingly random events in a chaotic world. We need to accept that some things are out of our control. Sometimes we take an undesirable event that is emotional enough, and then add stress and turmoil to it by relentlessly searching for the "why". This slows down the amount of time it takes to recover from an event.

To deny ourselves a grieving process when something bad happens is not healthy. We need to go through the process so that we can put the event behind us. Once we have experienced it long enough, then we can start to reframe our thoughts and move on from them.

If we feel bad, then allow ourselves to feel bad, but we don't need to turn it into misery or martyrdom. Accept that some things are out of our control, and then let nature take its course. Our minds are amazing and have a natural order in which they heal themselves. If we simply get out of our own way, our minds will lead us down the path to healing.

Pain is inevitable, misery is optional. Acceptance is a hard thing to learn, but when we practice acceptance and learn to let go, we experience greater peace and the ability to move on.

... grant me the serenity to accept the things I cannot change; the courage to change the things I can; and wisdom to know the difference.

Sound familiar?

Questions for discussion and reflection:

- Reflect and share an experience when I have practiced acceptance.
- Identify something that I may be holding onto that may be best to let go.
- What other skills can I use while Practicing Acceptance?
- What are some small ways I can practice this skill to help with harder times?

Skill: Understanding Impermanence

Remind myself that nothing is constant and these hard times will pass; things will get better.

Education: There is an old adage that time heals all wounds. Everything changes. The bad news is "nothing is permanent". The good news is "nothing is permanent".

A quote from Pema Chodron:

"Nothing is static or fixed, that all is fleeting and impermanent, is the first mark of existence. It is the ordinary state of affairs. Everything is in process. Every tree, every blade of grass, all the animals, insects, human beings, buildings, the animate and the inanimate are always changing, moment to moment."

"Change is inevitable, yet we react to change in a variety of ways. For some, change can be frightening, scary, or sad. For others, change can be exciting or joyous. Sometimes we welcome change, other times we resist it."

"This skill is useful during difficult times. Trust that this experience will pass. Use other skills of calming self, reframing, practicing acceptance."

"This skill can help with cravings. Ride the wave, focus on calming skills or choose to distract ourselves until the urge passes. Some people tell themselves they will just put using off until a later time (procrastinate) knowing that if they delay use long enough, the urge or craving will pass."

Realizing that all things are impermanent will help us make it through whatever it is that we are suffering from. Feelings inevitably change. The one thing we always can have control over is what and where we focus our attention.

The following excerpts provide information about how mindfully observing an urge and allowing it to pass reduces activity in the brain areas involved in cravings.

How Mindfulness Makes the Brain Immune to Temptation[65]

The smokers received a brief training in a technique called "surfing the urge." Bowen explained to the smokers that urges always pass eventually, whether or not you give in to them. When they felt a strong craving, they should imagine the urge as a wave in the ocean. It would build in intensity, but ultimately crash and dissolve. The smokers were to picture themselves riding the wave, not fighting it but also not giving in to it. They were instructed to pay close attention to the urge to smoke, without trying to change it or get rid of it. What thoughts were going through their mind? What did the urge feel like in the body?

Mindfulness seems to provide some kind of inoculation when exposed to triggers.

The reduced cravings correlated with reduced activity in craving-related areas of the brain (e.g. the anterior cingulate cortex). Interestingly, mindfulness didn't just reduce activity; it functionally disconnected the different regions of the brain that make up the "craving network."

Paying mindful attention to the trigger of the craving interrupted this complex brain response, and ultimately protected smokers from their own desire.

Understand impermanence, everything changes.

Questions for discussion and reflection:

- What are circumstances where this skill may be useful?
- What other skills can I use when I am practicing impermanence?
- What are some things I can learn to let go of?
- Share a story of when I have used this skill.
- Try a guided activity of surfing the urge.

---

[65] McGonigal, K. (2011) *The Science of Willpower*, *"How Mindfulness Makes the Brain Immune to Temptation"*.

Skill: Practicing Attached Detachment

Do my very best in life and then let go of the outcomes. Keep things in perspective.

Education: This skill has roots in Eastern ideas about detachment, and the premise that suffering comes from desire. This skill is the counter-balance of practicing acceptance. We accept, but we must also act. Without meaning, our lives can feel empty. Appreciate the value of not getting attached to things beyond our control, and at the same time, participating fully in life. All we can do is our best, and then what happens, happens.

This skill calls for showing up fully in life. It is the opposite of being complacent or passive. Understandably there will be some good days and some bad days, but step back and look over the landscape of your life and ask yourself, "Am I putting my heart and soul into my life?"

For example, a new business owner of an addiction program puts all their energy, financial resources, and heart into making it go. With so much invested, they could spend a lot of time worrying about all the things that could go wrong; liability, clients making self-defeating decisions, serious harm or safety considerations. In other words, they could live in a state of constant anxiety/worry. An alternative? Work hard, give it their very best, and then let go. Bad things happen, but they live each day trusting that no matter what happens, they can handle it.

Worrying does not produce positive results. It consumes energy, and when we are in stress mode, we do not have energy for positive growth. Having an anxious/fear-based perspective doesn't improve the circumstances, in fact, it only makes them worse.

Questions for discussion and reflection:

- Am I doing the best that I can? How can I be more trusting?
- If not, what I can do differently to feel like I am doing my best?
- How much of my energy do I spend worrying? How can I learn to let go?
- What things are truly within my control?
- Do I trust that no matter what happens, I will find my way?

Skill: Focusing on Effectiveness

Pay attention to the goal, and if needed, put aside pride or stubbornness and do what works. Be effective.

Education: Sometimes we can get caught up in an emotion and feel driven to behave accordingly, even if it means acting in a way that only makes things worse, or moves us farther from our goal. The purpose of this skill is to be aware of what we are trying to accomplish, and set aside emotions that may be interfering.

Some examples of this include feeling too prideful to ask for help, feeling ashamed and avoiding a situation, feeling hurt and allowing an important relationship to suffer, being stubborn and unwilling to give in despite knowing better, or being fearful to try something new.

Common feelings that tend to get in our way include fear, pride, stubbornness, hurt, anger, guilt, shame, and embarrassment. Would I rather be right or be happy?

Put another way. How many of us repeat the same arguments with our partner or our spouse? We put more energy into being right than getting what we need in the first place.

When these situations arise, try to think about the big picture, what really matters. It may be helpful to do a pros and cons list about taking a different course of action. This does not mean we give up our integrity or violate our values to get what we want. It does mean we balance our values with our needs and we focus on being effective.

Role plays are useful tools to practice acting in new and effective ways despite the discomfort.

Remember to use self-calming skills of breathing and mindfulness to help engage our frontal lobe and reduce the power of our emotion centers.

Questions for discussion and reflection:

- Recall a time when I let my emotions "run the show". What happened? Reflecting back, how could I have handled it differently?

- Why is it so difficult to control our emotions?

- What situations are the most difficult for me? Do I have any patterns?

- What are some personality traits that help make using this skill more likely?

- What other skills do I use when I practice being effective?

- How does this skill include the skill of Demonstrating Understanding?

- Role play various scenarios that tend to get us in trouble.

Skill: Demonstrating Understanding

People are more likely to listen to me if I first demonstrate that I HEAR THEM.

Education: Poor communication is often the cause of conflicts, power struggles, frustration, and relationship issues. This skill is the most essential communication tool that exists. In order to be effective with others, we need to be able to both listen and communicate our wants and needs. This skill focuses on communicating to another person that we accurately hear what they are telling us.

If we become effective at demonstrating that we hear people, they are more likely to feel comfortable with us and want to talk with us. If we are able to demonstrate understanding, people will be less prone to argue, and more willing to listen. Problem solving may be indicated at times, but most often, people prefer to just be heard. If the circumstances seem to warrant advice giving, first consider asking the person if he or she is interested in suggestions.

Another way to describe this skill is showing empathy. It communicates that we understand how others feel, that we can see things from their eyes. It does not mean that we have to agree with what they are saying. It simply means we hear what they are saying.

It is a gift to be understood. It feels validating. When this occurs, we are more likely to listen to the other person as well.

This is not problem solving, advice giving, or personalizing. This skill requires active listening (paying attention), asking open-ended questions (questions that require answers other than yes or no) to gather more information, and then repeating back what was heard (ideally not word for word).

An easy formula for practicing this skill is to listen to someone and then reply with:

"You feel _____ because _____".
            Feeling word   Reason for the feeling

It may seem awkward or artificial at first, but with practice our responses will come naturally and with greater ease. Practice whenever we have the opportunity, and see how it impacts our relationships.

Example: A friend tells you he had a hard day at work due to problems with a co-worker not showing up and needing to do double the work and then not getting any support from his boss and other co-workers. A response could be: "You feel unappreciated because you are doing all the work."

Following is a list of feelings that can be used to practice responding.

Happy	Positive	Uneasy	Unhappy	Frightened	Angry
pleased	determined	nervous	hurt	uneasy	frustrated
glad	forgiving	tense	upset	weak	cross
wonderful	hopeful	anxious	lonely	insecure	irritated
elated	motivated	flustered	miserable	inadequate	annoyed
excited	daring	insecure	bereft	tense	furious
content	energetic	angry	despairing	anxious	livid
surprised	loving	cross	devastated	nervous	enraged
proud	eager	confused	lost	scared	hurt
relieved	excited	bored	down	petrified	inadequate
satisfied	receptive	flat	depressed	threatened	trapped
confident	happy	apathetic	low	trapped	tired
hopeful	caring	weak	grief	used	scared
peaceful	confident	surprised	sad	despairing	embarrassed
comfortable	assertive	uncomfortable	rejected	miserable	used
calm	hopeful	lonely		lonely	jealous
relaxed	strong	discontented		shocked	overburdened
warm	vital	foolish		terrified	put upon
overjoyed		stupid		ashamed	pissed-off
love		confused			miffed
grateful		uncertain			disgusted
		worried			contempt
					aggrieved

Questions for discussion and reflection:

How can I become a better listener?

- Look at the feelings list and role play taking turns telling a story and have the other person share an empathy response.
- What are some examples of open-ended (versus closed) questions?
- What are examples of body language that show we are paying attention?
- Why do we tend to want to problem-solve/give advice?
- What does it mean to personalize something? How do we avoid doing this?

Skill: Developing Meaningful Activity

Find something to do that gives my life meaning and purpose.

Education: Everybody needs to have a purpose. A brilliant man who had been trained as a physicist, but later experienced a very disabling form of schizophrenia and was now doing clerical work, one day said to me, "I really appreciate having this job to come to each day. I don't care what it is, but everybody needs something in his life that gives him some meaning and purpose. It could be playing the guitar, caring for plants, a pet, or spending time with a friend. It does not need to be grand; in fact, the small things can have great significance."

Reward deficiency, or lack of worthwhile opportunities, increases the need for immediate gratification. It is important to build in rewards to satisfy our ever-hungry reward circuitry. Even small positive actions every day increase dopamine and change neural structures that add to large changes over time.

Following ancient wisdom, science is discovering we are hardwired for connection and compassion. Hope is an essential ingredient. Where do we find hope? Hope comes from experiencing a connection with another. It may be the connection to the program, to the staff, or to the other participants, that provide a reason for living. This connection is a first step, and small steps can be the beginning of a foundation. With a foundation, many things are possible. Success breeds success.

Material things do not give life meaning and purpose. It is the connections with others, helping those in need, spending time with people we love, being in nature, hobbies we enjoy, accomplishing goals, and of course, having fun.

A couple of quotes from *Tuesdays with Morrie*:

"So many people walk around with a meaningless life. They seem half asleep, even when they are busy doing things they think are important. This is because they're chasing the wrong things. The way you get meaning into your life is to devote yourself to loving others, devote yourself to your community around you, and devote yourself to creating something that gives you purpose and meaning."

"If you're trying to show off for people at the top, forget it. They will look down at you anyhow. And if you're trying to show off for people at the bottom, forget it. They will only envy you. Status will get you nowhere. Only an open heart will allow you to float equally between everyone."

Many years ago, a man struggled with whether life was worth living. He had a long history of suicidal behavior. Slowly over a couple of years, he started to add some small things into his daily routine. He started tending to plants, he joined a church, he started going to a self-help group. Granted, there were still days when he struggled, but he reported a greater sense of hope and he demonstrated a willingness to try new things. Brick by brick....

Questions for discussion and reflection:

- How can I discover or rediscover what I really want/believe/enjoy?
- What currently gives my life meaning and purpose?
- What motivates us to get up each day and put one foot in front of the other?
- What does it mean to love well?
- What changes do I need to make in my life to feel like I am living fully?
- How can I improve my connections with others?
- Discuss the meaning of hope.
- Discuss the idea of quality over quantity.
- What do we value? What are our values?

This chapter has provided information and handouts for skills training. A key theme in most of the skills is mindfulness and self-calming. Greater self-awareness, mindfulness, and the ability to observe and change thought patterns are powerful tools to help quiet our reward circuitry. The following chapter explains more about meditation and provides guided meditations that can be used as part of the treatment process.

Chapter Seven

Meditation

Meditation is a core element of the treatment process. While some clients may initially resist, at the time of program completion, they often identify it as one of the most satisfying treatment experiences. Anxiety is a very common reason people use drugs or alcohol. Many people report difficulty with racing or obsessive thoughts, sleep problems, or unease with social settings. Meditation is a useful intervention to train people to calm themselves and to slow or change their thoughts.

The primary goal of meditation is to learn how to use breathing for calming and to increase self-awareness regarding our own thoughts. Learning to observe our thoughts teaches us that we do not need to attach to them and we have the power to change them. This simple understanding of knowing that we can change our thoughts empowers us to become more mindful and self-aware, and increase self-control. We are less prone to knee-jerk reactions and we feel a greater sense of calm.

According to *The Practical Neuroscience of Buddha's Brain*[66], neurologists have determined that meditation can lead to the following benefits:

- Increases gray matter in the insula, hippocampus, and prefrontal cortex

- Reduces cortical thinning

- Improves psychological functions associated with the regions mentioned above, including attention, compassion, and empathy

- Increases activation in left frontal regions, which lifts mood

- Increases the power and reach of gamma-range brainwaves in experienced Tibetan practitioners. (Brain waves are measurable waves produced by large numbers of neurons firing rhythmically together.)

- Decreases stress-related cortisol

- Strengthens the immune system

- Helps a variety of medical conditions, including cardiovascular disease, asthma, type (2) diabetes, premenstrual syndrome (PMS), and chronic pain

- Helps numerous psychological conditions including insomnia, anxiety, phobias, and eating disorders

---

[66] Hanson, R., Mendius, R. (2009) *The Practical Neuroscience of Buddha's Brain.*

Meditation can be both easy and difficult. Starting is easy, as all it requires is some time and a quiet space. The difficulty is sticking to it. However, if we do it consistently, like most things, it gets much easier with practice. Like training a puppy, we are patient and loving as we keep bringing our mind back to our breath.

There are many ways to meditate. The following approach is one used at Minnesota Alternatives for focusing the mind. Repetition is essential for learning, so whatever method is used, it is helpful to repeat it over and over.

Focusing Your Mind:

1. Sit up straight, put your feet flat on the floor. Roll around your neck and shoulders and try to work out any tension you may be feeling in your body.

2. Take a deep breath into the base of your lungs. Feel your diaphragm push down causing your stomach to expand as you breathe in. Continue to breathe deeply, bringing air into the base of your lungs, stomach expanding as the breath comes in.

3. From the seat of an observer, watch what is going on in your mind. Separate from your thoughts and just watch them. And breathe. (Long pause.)

4. When thoughts appear, notice them, label them (for example: "work, family, food", and let them float away like a cloud passing in the sky or a leaf floating down a river. Just let them pass. (Allow 2 to 3 minutes for thought watching/labeling.)

5. As your thoughts quiet, notice the space that exists between your thoughts. (Long pause.)

6. If your thoughts are still coming, repeat the words "quiet mind" over and over and connect to your breathing.

7. Now we will sit quietly for several minutes and practice quieting our minds and noticing the space between thoughts. (Pause 6 to 8 minutes.)

8. Okay, let's come back now. Take a couple of more deep breaths. Wiggle your fingers and your toes. Slowly open your eyes and come on back.

My personal experience: Like anything, it takes practice. Do not get discouraged if it seems like your thoughts are impossible to slow down. My routine is to meditate first thing in the morning when I feel more calm and quiet, before the activity of the day begins. I lay flat in my bed (I find it easier to meditate lying down as I am less distracted by body discomfort) and focus on my breathing. I take a few deep breaths and start to watch my thoughts, but am now able to move fairly quickly into "stopping my thoughts." I then just hang out in the "space between the thoughts".

Removing barriers increases my willingness to practice. Do what you can to make it easy to try.

While meditating, one of four things is happening:

- I am totally immersed in my thoughts (fueling them).
- I am labeling them (work, work, work, work) and then letting them pass like a leaf floating down a river. (Yes, all work and no play makes Paula a dull girl.)
- I am not thinking (per se), but I am working at not thinking by repeating "quiet mind" in my head.
- I am not thinking, and I am not working at not thinking, meaning I am in a calm and very peaceful state.

After several months of practice, people report a greater sense of calm, lowered tendency to emotional reactions, and a greater sense of contentment. Again, practice is essential and success develops over time.

Guided Meditations

A key part of the treatment process is staff-led guided meditation sessions. It generally happens in two parts. The first part is the meditation described above, called Focusing Your Mind, and the second is guided using one of following meditations. The staff is encouraged to bring their own ideas and meditations as long as they are consistent with the program skills. The following four guided meditations can be used to lead meditations in a group or in an individual session. These guided meditations help with focusing the mind and facilitating the following:

- Experiencing emotions
- Letting go
- Changing behavior
- Building positive experiences

Suggestions for guided meditations:

Each meditation should take about 10 minutes so allow plenty of pauses for people to quiet their minds and create the images. Feel free to ask the group members for input on which meditation they want/need that day. Please review these key points before you start.

Key Points:

- The brain is so powerful because it is so sensitive to experience. Where we focus our attention, defines us at a neurological level.
- Nerve cells that fire together, wire together. If we think the same thoughts and behave in the same ways, our brains become hard-wired, and the cells in the body become conditioned. Change becomes very difficult.

- If we want to change, we need to be very intentional and have novel or new experiences. We must change both thoughts AND actions. Repetition is essential.

- Meditation and imagery are powerful tools to create change. If we involve all five senses and create vivid images, our brains do not know whether or not it is really happening.

- The act of mental rehearsal is a powerful way to grow and mold new circuits in our brains. Practicing new ways of being when we are calm, helps us prepare for when we get triggered.

- When we stop upgrading the brain with new information, it becomes hardwired, riddled with automatic programs of behavior.

- The goal is to interrupt negative habitual thought processes before they produce painful chemicals in the body. Can we become more aware of our thoughts?

Experiencing Emotions

Experience emotions as body sensations. Consider them as waves of sensation that peak and then subside. Let go of the story line, focus on your breathing, stay with the experience, trusting it will pass. Learning to feel emotions in your body allows you to step away from them.

1. Sit up straight, put your feet flat on the floor, roll around your neck and shoulders and try to work out any tension you may be feeling in your body.

2. Take a deep breath into the base of your lungs. Feel your diaphragm push down causing your stomach to expand as you breathe in. Continue to breathe deeply, bringing air into the base of your lungs, stomach expanding as the breath comes in.

3. Focus on your breathing...your mind starts to quiet.

4. Start by naming a painful or negative emotion that is holding you back. Give it a name and speak the name of the emotion in your mind.

5. Breathe.

6. As you name the emotion, feel it in your body. How does it feel? Where in your body do you feel it? Feel all the sensations that you can. Name the sensations... notice the feeling as it rises like a wave...and breathe.

7. While breathing, step away from the story. Allow the sensations in your body.

8. Stay with the sensations until you feel them start to subside or mellow.

9. Continue to sit quietly. When the emotion lets up, take a couple of deep breaths and slowly open your eyes and come on back.

Letting Go[67]

Holding onto resentments and anger can keep you from living life fully or to your greatest potential. Learning to forgive and let go does not mean you are approving or condoning the behavior. It means you are choosing to free yourself from the negative and toxic effects that these feelings can create.

1. Sit up straight, put your feet flat on the floor, roll around your neck and shoulders, and try to work out any tension you may be feeling in your body.

2. Take a deep breath into the base of your lungs. Feel your diaphragm push down causing your stomach to expand as you breathe in. Continue to breathe deeply; bringing air into the base of your lungs, stomach expanding as the breath comes in.

3. Focus on your breathing…your mind starts to quiet.

4. To begin, think about a time when you were forgiven for something you did. Picture yourself saying you are sorry. Visualize the person accepting your apology. Remember how this made you feel.

5. Now bring to mind someone or something that you have been holding onto that you know is not good for you. It could be someone that has harmed you or abandoned you. It could be God, or a higher power. It could be yourself, a regret that you feel for things you have done.

6. Remember to breathe; feel your stomach expand as you breathe in.

7. Now use imagery to shrink the person involved. Make the person so small that he or she is not a threat to you or anyone. You scoop this small being into your hand.

8. You see the person crying and asking for forgiveness and offering you an explanation.

9. You notice how sad and little he or she is.

10. Hear the person's explanation…understand more of his or her story…what has happened in the person's life…

11. Feel yourself begin to soften… and breathe.

12. You begin to develop an understanding. Holding onto these feelings only hurts you. You are letting them go. Feel your resentment and anger start to melt away.

13. Continue to breathe and notice these feelings fade away.

14. When you are ready, take a couple of deep breaths and slowly open your eyes and come on back.

---

[67] Barrash, J., Discovery of Self – The Continuum Center, Minneapolis MN.

Changing Behavior[68]

Use imagery and mental rehearsal to change how you think and how you behave. "Nerve cells that fire together wire together". If you think the same thoughts and behave in the same ways, your brain becomes hard-wired and the cells in the body become conditioned making change more difficult. Train your body and your brain to a new set of circumstances – break old patterns, and be open to new and novel experiences.

1. Sit up straight, put your feet flat on the floor, roll around your neck and shoulders, and try to work out any tension you may be feeling in your body.

2. Take a deep breath into the base of your lungs. Feel your diaphragm push down causing your stomach to expand as you breathe in. Continue to breathe deeply, bringing air into the base of your lungs, stomach expanding as the breath comes in.

3. Focus on your breathing…your mind starts to quiet.

4. Now identify a behavior that you want to change. Give it a name and speak it out in your mind. Speak it out again. Become familiar with it. Notice how your body feels and how you are acting. Put yourself fully into the old behavior engaging all your senses. What do you see? Notice colors, textures, sounds, smells.

5. Now imagine a new way of being. Change your personality and change your reality. Visualize yourself making different choices, reacting in different ways…living in a way that reflects your true self. Again, put yourself fully into this new behavior engaging all your senses. What do you see? Notice colors, textures, sounds, smells. Mentally rehearse this new way of thinking and behaving over and over.

6. Now I want you to return to your old way of thinking and behaving. Think about an event or trigger that causes you to behave in this old way. See yourself in this situation, but before you act in the same old ways, tell yourself to breathe, slow down, and STOP.

7. And again practice your new way of being. Change your personality and change your reality. Visualize yourself making different choices, reacting in different ways…living in a way that reflects your true self. Be moved by the power within you to change. Mentally rehearse this new way of behaving, showing the courage and determination to change.

8. Now gently bow your head and give thanks for any help you receive to create a new way of being. Open your heart and feel the gratitude for these changes.

9. When you are ready, take a couple of deep breaths and slowly open your eyes and come on back.

---

[68] Dispenza, J. (2007) *Evolve Your Brain: The Science of Changing Your Mind.*

Building Positive Experiences

Positive imagery helps to create new neural networks built on positive thoughts and actions so your brain patterns are not so easily drawn to existing negative networks. Positive emotions release dopamine and dopamine not only makes us happy, it turns on the learning centers of the brain.

1. Sit up straight, put your feet flat on the floor, roll around your neck and shoulders, and try to work out any tension you may be feeling in your body.

2. Take a deep breath into the base of your lungs. Feel your diaphragm push down causing your stomach to expand as you breathe in. Continue to breathe deeply, bringing air into the base of your lungs, stomach expanding as the breath comes in.

3. Focus on your breathing…your mind starts to quiet.

4. First bring to mind one of your favorite memories. What do you see? Notice colors, textures, sounds, smells.

5. Next bring to mind a time in your life when you felt true joy. What do you see? Notice colors, textures, sounds, smells.

6. Speak these messages in your mind: I am filled with loving kindness. I am well. I am peaceful and at ease. And I am happy.

7. Next bring to mind something or someone you are grateful for. A friend, a family member, someone you know, an experience, a small miracle, a blessing…now gently bow your head and give thanks.

8. You understand a grateful heart is a healthy heart.

9. When you are ready, take a couple of deep breaths and slowly open your eyes.

Meditation is a daily core treatment activity and most clients report finding it very helpful. Copies of the guided meditations can be purchased and downloaded from the Minnesota Alternatives website or a CD can be sent in the mail.

Chapter Eight

Other Considerations

This chapter addresses other considerations that include mental health, youth and young adults, and residential program strategies. Minnesota Alternatives specializes in working with clients who may experience mental illness and also serves many young people who are new to adulthood. Residential treatment is not provided, but due to many years of residential experience, I devoted a section to program strategies.

Mental Health and Trauma-Informed Care

This section provides an overview of some mental health strategies to use when working with people who have co-occurring mental health and substance use issues. It builds on previous information about key skills, mindfulness, self-calming, reframing thoughts and behaviors and brain education.

SAMHSA (Substance Abuse and Mental Health Services Administration)[69] lists the central attitudes or skills needed by staff when working with co-occurring disorders:

- Develop a therapeutic alliance
- Work from a recovery perspective
- Monitor client psychiatric symptoms
- Use motivational enhancement related to client stage of change
- Use behavioral techniques to address behaviors
- Use skill building and repetition to target deficits
- Adopt an attitude of client responsibility for his or her own recovery
- Help clients recognize existing strengths and build on them
- Exude a sense of hope for the client and his or her recovery

According to the SAMSHA, the following are evidence-based practices for co-occurring disorders:

- Motivational Interviewing
- Cognitive-behavioral therapy

---

[69] SAMHSA Treatment Improvement Protocol #42, *Substance Abuse Treatment for Persons with Co-Occurring Disorders.*

- Stage-wise treatment
- Relapse prevention
- Knowledge of psychotropic medications

Mental health knowledge and experience is essential. Many clients have co-occurring disorders, including serious and persistent mental illnesses, such as bi-polar disorder, schizoaffective disorder, schizophrenia, major depression, and personality disorders. It is important to understand and practice trauma-informed care and have a basic understanding about psychotropic medications. Many clients take medications as part of their recovery from both substance use and mental health disorders.

The basics of behavioral theory should be understood, and staff must pay attention to what behaviors are being reinforced. It is important to celebrate success and be very mindful to reinforce positive behaviors and strive to not reinforce negative behaviors. This requires mindfulness, as it is natural to give a lot of energy to problematic behaviors. Staff may need to remind each other about what behaviors they are reinforcing.

Crisis plans are useful for identifying triggers, high-risk situations, symptoms, and skills/tools/supports that can be used in response. Many clients benefit from making agreements or contracts to provide external motivation and accountability. Diet, nutrition, basic self-care and exercise are essential for improved mental health.

Clients should be referred for psychiatric evaluation and possibly psychotropic medications when indicated.

It can be difficult to know what may be drug/alcohol interactions or withdrawal as these symptoms mirror many mental illnesses. The information below includes differential diagnosis information to help sort this out, but it takes drug-free time and knowledge about each client's history to gain a clear understanding.

The sections below also include interventions specific to various mental health issues:

Anxiety – Anxiety may be increased or decreased by drugs and alcohol. Panic attacks can be induced by either acute cocaine ingestion or opioid withdrawal. Alcohol withdrawal also causes prominent anxiety. Ensure the person is not medically at risk, and if needed, educate him or her about the symptoms/risks of withdrawal. The majority of clients who present for treatment report difficulty with anxiety and identify this as a primary motive for use. Focus on diaphragmatic breathing and mindfulness. Practicing breathing with the client and watch him or her to make sure the breathing is being done properly. Medications can be useful, but emphasize the benefits of learning skills for self-calming. Allow for "time outs," and understand that groups can be very difficult for people who are anxious. Offer soothing activities (i.e., art, journaling, music, Reiki, massage) and let people do these when needed rather than being in group all the time. The program may need to primarily focus on 1:1 time and slow engagement until the person has learned calming skills.

Depression – Many clients report problems with depression. During withdrawal it can be caused by either sedatives or stimulants and usually resolves in 2 to 3 weeks. Some depression may last for a few months. Clients with depressive symptoms benefit from the skill of enhancing positive experiences, deliberately working to establish new neural networks based on gratitude, positive memories, and acts of compassion. Clients who are depressed need hope and encouragement. Their lives often lack meaning. They may need a lot of structure and accountability (external motivators) to help them get out of bed and show up. Others many need flexibility and outreach, with engagement as the priority. Help them learn to appreciate the small things and focus on cultivating hope.

Thought Disorders – Schizophrenia is often misdiagnosed in stimulant abusers. Toxicology results are essential as are longitudinal assessments while drug free. Persons with schizophrenia are often highly sensitive to most drugs and will exhibit substantial symptoms with small amounts of drugs. Opioid and alcohol use may reduce symptoms temporarily, whereas withdrawal will make them worse.

People with schizophrenia or schizoaffective disorders generally do well in this setting due to the welcoming and flexible structure. It is important that they feel comfortable sharing about the symptoms they experience. Mental health education helps others understand the illness and allows for open discussion. There are some good films (*A Beautiful Mind*, *The Soloist*) that are useful educational tools.

Many clients struggle with medication compliance due to the side effects, and they often work to reduce or discontinue them. Clients are encouraged to work with their prescriber to find medication they can tolerate and ideally be on the lowest dose necessary to maintain stability. Staff needs to validate the difficulty of side effects.

A primary intervention for people with thought disorders includes developing a list of their warning signs so they know if their symptoms are becoming problematic. Teach them to monitor their own symptoms based on this list so they can seek intervention if needed. Many clients choose to tolerate symptoms and use only minimal medications. This requires good self-care, stress management, planning for stressful times, support to seek "reality checks", and skillful use of calming techniques. Clients learn to identify "common psychotic thoughts" and teach themselves to not act when these thoughts occur. Mindfulness helps them stay in the present and calm themselves.

Clients with thought disorders often comment that they enjoy the meditation exercises and find them useful. According to a recent study, fifteen individuals diagnosed with schizophrenia spectrum disorders participated in a pilot study testing a mindfulness-based intervention to reduce anxiety. Outcomes mentioned most frequently by participants were relaxation, relief from psychological symptoms, cognitive changes, and being able to focus on the present. Results suggested that mindfulness meditation training was acceptable to all participants; no one reported worsening of psychotic or other symptoms while meditating.[70]

Bi-Polar Disorder – Mania can be induced by stimulants and may be an exacerbation of bipolar disorder. There is no good way to tell the difference except by history. The person should be assessed when drug free.

Clients need to learn about the symptoms of mania and depression. This allows them to identify their warning signs and then self-monitor. It is important for clients to learn about triggers or situations that can aggravate their symptoms. Some report seasonal variations, and need to practice extra care during certain times of the year. Medications can be very helpful, but can also trigger episodes of mania so clients are encouraged to work with their prescribers to find medications they can tolerate and ideally be on the lowest doses necessary to maintain stability. Skills training is essential for coping strategies and self-care. Mindfulness helps with staying in the present and self-calming.

Post-Traumatic Stress Disorder (PTSD) – The vast majority of women and more than half the men in treatment report histories of sexual abuse.[71] Staff understands and practices trauma-informed care that includes:

- Understanding that people are not always able to communicate their trauma histories.

- Programs wish to not do further harm.

- Therapeutic alliance is essential. Develop trust. Dignity and respect should be emphasized.

- Understanding that staff-imposed rules, and rule enforcement is conflict-generating, and rules eliminate the need to think and problem solve.

- Recognize that coercive interventions cause traumatization and are to be avoided.

- Retelling of the stories can be re-traumatizing. Clinicians need to monitor arousal and teach clients to decrease distress (self-soothe).

EMDR: Minnesota Alternatives employs a therapist who specializes in EMDR (Eye Movement Desensitization and Reprocessing), which is a therapy that allows the client to

---

[70] Brown, L., Davis, L., LaRocco, V., Strasburger, A. (2010) *American Journal of Psychiatric Rehabilitation*, 13:3, 224-242, "Participant Perspectives on Mindfulness Meditation Training for Anxiety in Schizophrenia".

[71] Plummer, J. (2005) *Substance abuse treatment capacity: Childhood physical and sexual abuse and neglect has a staggering impact on the prevalence of substance abuse in adulthood: current treatment capacity is inadequate to meet the need.* Unpublished manuscript.

address issues of trauma in a more private way. The therapist isn't made aware of the specific details of the trauma, which is typically the worst part of the traumatic memory. The client is able to address the trauma on his or her terms, without the fear of full disclosure, which is common in more traditional therapies.

Trauma often manifests itself in the form of anxiety, panic, flashbacks, and depression. Benzodiazepines, alcohol, marijuana, and other substances of abuse are known to effectively medicate these symptoms, which make reducing or quitting these substances much more of a challenge for people with unresolved trauma.

Before the trauma is addressed, the therapist and the client work on identifying a Safe Place. This is where the client employs mindfulness and meditation skills to find a "place" in his or her mind that feels safe. The client is asked to use all five senses and imagery, which helps promote a sense of calm. This activity is to be used in response to emotions that cause stress, anxiety, and overwhelm. The Safe Place activity skill provides control when negative/difficult feelings emerge. It is a key skill, and when firmly established, recovery progress can be expected.

EMDR uses bi-lateral stimulation as memories of trauma are recalled. People who have gone through EMDR often say after just a few sessions that the trauma is "a bit fuzzier than it used to be", making details and feelings less accessible, therefore reducing the power of the trauma. Many people who have experienced EMDR try to recall the trauma, and often say something like, "I can't seem to remember as clearly as I did before, or the memory seems to have a haze over it".

The progressive telling of the traumatic experience in the presence of another person who is caring, soothing, and protective allows the hippocampus to reactivate implicit (habits, emotional reactions, mostly midbrain and cerebellum) free-floating memory fragments and re-store them into explicit (consciously retrieved at will, neocortex) memory, creating a coherent life story that relieves the emotional stress of trauma and allows a new, more secure attachment bond to develop.[72]

Positive experiences can be used to soothe, balance, and even replace negative ones. When two thoughts are held in the mind at the same time, they start to connect with each other. The process of building memory provides the opportunity to shift the emotional shadings of your interior landscape. Every time you shift positive feelings/views into painful states of mind, you build neural structure (Hanson, R., Mendius, R., 2009).

---

[72] Siegel, D. J. (2010). *Mindsight: The new science of personal transformation.* New York: Bantam Books.

The Neurobiology of Trauma

Research suggests that trauma leads to a biphasic response in the brain, characterized by hyperresponsivity followed by numbing. During acute stress, the brain is flooded with norepinephrine triggering a constellation of physiological hyper-responses. The hyperresponse results in intrusive symptoms such as recurring thoughts of the trauma, hyperarousal, and an exaggerated startle response. The stress of long-term hyperarousal leads to depletion of norepinephrine and dopamine. High levels of stress hormones may result in damage to the hippocampus and subsequent memory problems.[73]

The second part of the biphasic response to stress includes symptoms of emotional numbing, deficits in learning, decreased motivation, and emotional constriction. Pain and traumatic stress cause a stress-induced analgesia as a result of the release of endorphins. The effects of long-term activation of the endogenous opioid systems result in impairment with memory, cognition, and reality testing and contribute to the emotional blunting and disassociation often seen in survivors of trauma.[74]

Opiate depletion can contribute to risk-taking behaviors. For example, self-harm behaviors can be a response to depletion in the endogenous opioid system from chronic over-activation. Self-inflicted pain reawakens the system causing endorphins to be released. The implications for narcotic addiction are obvious.[75]

Borderline Personality Disorders – Working with people with borderline personality disorders (BPD) requires a skillful balance of validation and expectation for change. Dialectical Behavioral Therapy (DBT) has shown to be helpful, but many clients have already completed DBT. Some clients are unable to complete the process, which often takes up to a year or longer. Many clients report they find the skills confusing. The skills taught at Minnesota Alternatives are easy to understand, brief, and they can be learned in a short period of time. They are very useful for people who have BPD to help with self-care/boundaries, self-calming, reframing, and becoming more effective.

It is essential to cultivate an understanding that people are responsible for their own safety and sobriety. Be clear and consistent that it is not the staff's responsibility to keep people safe and sober. We can coach, support, reinforce and teach skills, but ultimately clients decide what they are going to do. Talk with clients about the locus of control. Only if someone poses a serious safety threat to self or others, will staff intervene and assume the locus of control. This may include use of emergency services, hospitalization, or a crisis program. When a client is struggling, staff needs to be empathic and encourage skill use,

---

[73] Denning, P., Little, J. (2012) *Practicing Harm Reduction Psychotherapy* 2nd Edition. (p.205).
[74] Cozolino, L. (2010) The neuroscience of psychotherapy: Healing the social brain (2nd ed.) New York: Norton.
[75] Denning, P., Little, J. (2012) *Practicing Harm Reduction Psychotherapy* 2nd Edition. (p.206).

but also be mindful of when the client is trying to make his or her problem "your" problem. Supervision and consultation are important to help sort out where to draw boundaries and how to keep the locus of control with the client. This is a very important consideration, especially when working with Axis II behaviors as some behaviors involve self-injury, but may not pose a serious risk.

It is very effective to have candid, respectful conversations with clients who experience BPD regarding safety and locus of control. It is a way to role model direct communication and boundaries. It helps to engage them as partners in their recovery and sends a message of empowerment: that they can be trusted to learn skills and practice self-care.

A very useful resource for co-occurring disorders is David Mee-Lee, M.D. He is a leading expert in co-occurring substance use and mental disorders and he authors a monthly online newsletter. "Tips and Topics", now in its tenth year of publication, explores subjects and solutions drawn from over 30 years of experience in person-centered treatment and program development.

It can be found at the website listed below.

http://changecompanies.net/tipsntopics/tag/david-mee-lee/

Cognitive Deficits

Minnesota Alternatives does not specialize in serving people with cognitive deficits, but the program strives to individualize services and difficulty with learning is not a barrier for admission. The program offers flexible scheduling, so shorter sessions can help with attention and tolerance challenges. The program can emphasize 1:1 counseling versus group services to give people a chance to gain skills and perhaps join groups at a later time.

For example, clients who have a difficult time in groups may come only for short sessions, and be allowed to work on projects alone while group sessions may be going on elsewhere.

The low-key and welcoming environment is helpful for people who are sensitive to stimulation. Peers can also be engaged to help each other if someone needs additional attention. Skills training is individualized to reflect the learning needs of the client and a variety of teaching techniques are used to help the client generalize the skills into his or her daily life.

Chronic Pain

Chronic Pain is a challenging issue. Clients who use narcotic pain medication should not be denied access to treatment, as they often are in conventional programs. Clients who suffer from chronic pain often misuse opiate medications due to tolerance issues as well as the desire to mood alter. Pain management is complicated, and referrals to pain clinics can help ensure a comprehensive assessment combined with alternative pain management strategies. Close coordination with the medical professionals involved in the client's care can help reduce excessive prescribing.

It is important to educate clients about the risks of overdose. Set treatment goals that are meaningful and relevant, and encourage self-monitoring of use, with a goal to reduce harm and/or use.

It can be very helpful to have a family member or support person monitor and dispense the use of opiates. Minnesota Alternatives does monitor medication, but this is not a long-term solution.

Strategies for pain management:

1. **Learn deep breathing or meditation to help with chronic pain.** Deep breathing and meditation are techniques that help the body relax, which eases pain. Tension and tightness release from muscles as they receive a quiet message to relax.

2. **Reduce stress.** Stress intensifies chronic pain. Negative feelings can increase the body's sensitivity to pain. Learning to take control of stress may provide some relief from chronic pain.

3. **Boost pain relief with the natural endorphins from exercise.** Endorphins are brain chemicals that help improve mood while also blocking pain signals. Exercise strengthens muscles, helping prevent re-injury and further pain.

4. **Alcohol can worsen sleep problems.** Pain makes sleep difficult, and alcohol can make sleep problems worse.

5. **Join a support group. Meet others living with chronic pain.** One feels less alone when with people who understand what it is like as well as benefiting from their wisdom about how to cope.

6. **Don't smoke.** It can worsen chronic pain. Smoking can worsen painful circulation problems and increase risk of heart disease and cancer.

7. **Track your pain level and activities every day.** Keep medical professionals informed. Keeping a log or journal of daily "pain score" will help track pain. At the end of each day, note the pain level on a scale of 1 to 10. Also, note what activities were done that day. Share the log with medical staff to provide a good understanding of pain issues and functioning level.

8. **Learn biofeedback to decrease pain severity.** Through biofeedback, it is possible to consciously control various body functions. There is good evidence that biofeedback works, and it is not that difficult to master.

9. **Use body work/massage for chronic pain relief.** Massage can help reduce stress, relieve tension, and speed the healing of injuries.

10. **Eat a healthy diet.** A well-balanced diet aids the digestive process, reduces heart disease risk, keeps weight under control, and improves blood sugar levels.

11. **Find ways to distract from pain.** Focusing on pain makes it worse rather than better. Instead, find something enjoyable to do that helps distract thoughts away from pain.

Pain may not be avoidable, but it does not need to control one's life.

Considerations for Youth and Young Adults

The model of treatment provided at Minnesota Alternatives is also a very good fit for young adults. It emphasizes brain development, which is essential for youth. The environment supports self-efficacy, empowerment and provides learning opportunities in self-regulation and impulse control. It provides skills training to help equip people with practical tools for many of life's challenges. Minnesota Alternatives is licensed to only work with adults, but serves many people who are ages 18 to 21.

There are many issues that need to be considered regarding youth. Excerpts from three articles effectively summarize some important considerations:

- *Kidnapped by Technology* addresses the impact of technology and the groundwork it lays for addictive behavior.

- *What's Wrong with the Teenage Mind?* addresses brain development.

- *Does Teen Drug Rehab Cure Addiction or Create It?* addresses substance use treatment considerations.

Technology and the Groundwork for Addictive Behavior

Children are experiencing much greater levels of stimulation than ever before. Kids are frequently seen absorbed in a game, on a hand-held or in-home gaming system, and they seem to prefer playing electronic games to almost any other activity.

Clinic visits for bipolar youth quadrupled between 1995 and 2003. What is happening?

A theory points to the high-stress, media-intensive environments in which kids are raised. Children's brains are "sculpted" by their experiences, particularly by emotional or intense experiences. The more children are exposed to stress, anxiety, and grief, the more their brains are hard-wired to react instinctively to emotional experiences, said Dr. L. Read Sulik, a child psychiatrist in Fargo, N.D. "Our kids today are by and large stimulated at a much higher level and stressed at a much higher level than before," he said. "We should be stepping back and saying: What is changing that we are seeing such an increase in the number of children that are having significant emotional and behavioral problems?"

From *Kidnapped By Technology*:

"When a child plays a computer game, each time they blow something or someone to bits, shoot down or destroy a plane, ship, UFO or any vehicle, break through a wall or barrier in order to move to the next level, or beat a character to severe injury, the brain responds chemically. In fact, it is proven that the pleasure center begins to release high amounts of dopamine, the brain's natural pleasure chemical."

"The bottom line is that dopamine makes us feel good, especially when we're winning at such a high pace. In addition, when accomplishment is coupled with excitement, the brain produces the adrenalines norepinephrine and epinephrine in order to wake itself up with a boost of heightened awareness. This chemical cocktail is the perfect mix for problems in normal brain function."

"To reiterate, this type of computer game stimulation is not so bad for a short run, but begins to cause problems in the long-term. As the brain's reward center is repeatedly activated and the strong chemicals are released during the gaming, pleasure zones become overstimulated. As a result, the reward system becomes desensitized and then recalibrates itself to a higher threshold. In other words, it will need more of a chemical rush to produce the same feelings. A side effect of this mechanism is addiction...and when it is tied to attention and learning, serious effects manifest."

"When a child's computer activity ends, one can expect the child to look like a drone because we're probably not all that interesting compared to what he or she has just been experiencing. In truth, everything in life will seem boring. Simple things like, playing with the dog or even visiting with a grandparent will seem like trivial nonsense. Why? Because nothing in the normal, mundane world can match the ecstasy of the virtual world or the super high it produces. Sounds like an addiction?"

"Without proper restraint, future choices may be married to things that produce more heightened stimulation: drugs, pornography, gambling, excess shopping, over-eating ... all because the brain's satiation center craves to be fulfilled (Dispenza 2009).[76]"

A couple of recent real life experiences illustrate this point:

- A young boy, who spends most of his day with electronic gaming, was taken to a swimming pool, and refused to participate claiming it was too boring. It is hard to imagine being a child and finding a trip to a swimming pool boring.

---

[76] Dispenza, J. (2009) *Kidnapped by Technology* at www.joedispenza.com.

- A six-year-old who spends most of his leisure time playing with his gaming system is told by his mother he needs to shut it off and get in the car to go to school. He becomes anxious at the idea of having to stop his game, and proceeds to scream and cry in a state of panic. Panic is stress. This is not good for young children, or anyone for that matter.

Newsweek Magazine (July 2012) includes an article about the use of the internet called "Is the onslaught making us crazy?" It concludes that studies show a connection between time spent online and mood disorders in young adulthood. Case Western Reserve University correlated heavy texting and social media use with stress, depression, and suicidal thinking.[77]

Brain Development

It is important to provide youth scientifically accurate information about the risks of using drugs and alcohol. It is especially critical to inform them that their brains are still developing and the "executive or CEO" part of the brain is the last part to develop. They need to understand the essential role this part of the brain plays in self-regulation, analytical thinking, executive functions, and decision making.

They need to be asked:

The command center of your brain is still developing, why would you want to take drugs or abuse alcohol and risk messing up the wiring of this essential area?

We know that the frontal lobe develops as youth age, but it also develops as it is needed. Excerpts from the following article highlight this point.

From *What's Wrong with the Teenage Mind?*

"There do seem to be many young adults who are enormously smart and knowledgeable but directionless, who are enthusiastic and exuberant, but unable to commit to a particular kind of work or a particular love until well into their 20s or 30s."

"First, experience shapes the brain. People often think that if some ability is located in a particular part of the brain that must mean that it's 'hard-wired' and inflexible. But, in fact, the brain is so powerful precisely because it is so sensitive to experience."

"It's as true to say that our experience of controlling our impulses make the prefrontal cortex develop as it is to say that prefrontal development makes us better at controlling our impulses. Our social and cultural life shapes our biology."

---

[77] *Newsweek Magazine* (July 18, 2012) *iCrazy: Panic. Depression. Psychosis. How connection addiction is rewiring our brains.*

"The new view of the adolescent brain isn't that the prefrontal lobes just fail to show up; it's that they aren't properly instructed and exercised."

"The brains of youth who are given opportunities to make decisions, to try new things, to learn to calm themselves down, to experience both the rewards and the natural consequences of their choices, develop accordingly (Gopnik, A 2012).[78]"

"Are we providing youth enough opportunities to "learn for themselves?" A new term has been coined called 'helicopter parents', so named because, like helicopters, they hover closely overhead, rarely out of reach, and attempt to sweep all obstacles out of the paths of their children."

"We need to provide opportunities for young adults to develop their big thinking brains, by giving them opportunities to think for themselves and learn from their experiences."

Treatment Considerations

Substance-abuse experts are finding that teen drug treatment may be doing more harm than good. Young adults or teens do not identify with the ideas of powerless and surrender. If anything, they seem to see themselves as indestructible.

From *Does Teen Drug Rehab Cure Addiction or Create It?*

"Many programs throw casual dabblers together with hard-core addicts and foster continuous group interaction. It tends to strengthen dysfunctional behavior by concentrating it, researchers say. 'Just putting kids in group therapy actually promotes greater drug use,' says Dr. Nora Volkow, director of the National Institute on Drug Abuse (NIDA)."

"It doesn't help either that the philosophy behind many drug-treatment programs can be easily misinterpreted by teenagers. Most programs in the U.S., are modeled after the 12-Step recovery plan used by Alcoholics Anonymous. The first step encourages participants to accept that they are 'powerless' over their addiction and to surrender their will to a higher force. For some people, it inspires mutual support and abstinence, but for others — especially teenagers — it can foster a feeling of defeat. 'You get these 12-Step teachings telling you that you're doomed, that you have this disease and this is the only way out,' Thomas says."

"Indeed, surrender is not a word that comes easily to teens, and teaching them to believe they are powerless may create a fatalism that leads to relapse, according to Andrew Morral,

---

[78] Gopnik, A. (2012) *The Wall Street Journal,* "What's Wrong With the Teenage Mind?"

a senior behavioral scientist at the Rand Corp. In his studies of teens treated at Phoenix House, one of the largest treatment providers in the U.S., he found that participants who subscribed to the tenet of powerlessness were more likely to return to drugs after treatment, compared with teenagers who did not take the message to heart."

"Still, for an estimated 10% of teen drug users whose addictions are severe enough that they already feel helpless to control them, the 12-Step method can help. For example, a study published in July in the journal Drug and Alcohol Dependence found that teens that had severe addictions to alcohol, marijuana, heroin, or painkillers and chose voluntarily to attend 12-Step meetings once a week for three months had nearly double the number of sober days as those who did not attend. "

"The problem is that most treatment programs do not give teens a choice about 12-Step attendance; it is usually a mandatory part of rehab or is in some cases legally mandated by a court."

"Although individual and family therapy have shown more success with teen drug users than group treatment, most programs continue to use problematic approaches. One reason is cost. Group treatment allows a therapist to see many more patients in a day than individual sessions would (Szalavitz, M 2010).[79]"

Most young adults that we have served do not embrace a lifelong goal of abstinence, but are motivated to reduce use or abstain from certain substances. They are very interested in the science of addiction and seem to have a lot of "a ha" moments when they learn what they are doing to their brains. Often they start treatment "misrepresenting" their use patterns. Once they know it is safe to be authentic, they start to open up and share honestly.

Residential Program Strategies

This practice guide is designed as a model for outpatient use; however it can be easily integrated into a residential setting.

Each residential program is unique and will have varying responses regarding resident substance use/abuse. Many residents may have a goal of abstinence, but staff understands that many residents are not at a stage of recovery to achieve abstinence and for some abstinence may not be their goal. These strategies can be used to work with residents who use substances while in treatment and ideally help to move the resident along in the process of change and/or reduce the harm resulting from the substance use.

---

[79] Szalavitz, M. (2010) *Time Magazine*, "Does Teen Drug Rehab Cure Addiction or Create It?"

A programs threshold for what can be tolerated changes based on current staff and resident composition. Teams and therapeutic communities go through varying levels of competence and unity, therefore the ability to manage more difficult behaviors changes as well. The ideal response is flexible and individualized based on the unique needs of the resident and the following considerations:

- Is the resident making progress or moving in a positive direction? Can you see a reduction in the use or the harm from the use?

- What are the legal issues? Is the resident under a commitment or probation/parole?

- What are the health considerations? Will continued use have a significant impact on the resident's health status?

- What is the context of the use? Is the resident using in less harmful ways? Involving others in the facility? Bringing drugs onto the property?

- How is the use impacting the milieu? Is it disrupting the therapeutic community?

- How is the use impacting the resident's ability to participate in treatment or meet his or her treatment obligations (i.e., pay room and board)?

Create a welcoming culture that communicates that you trust the residents to make good choices and handle responsibility (self-fulfilling prophecy). Keep rules to a minimum and give the clients as much control over the environment as possible. Put them in charge of chores, meals, and peer support. Again, avoid power struggles, and create a setting that "mirrors" independent living so they have opportunities to learn to trust themselves and practice self-regulation.

Define the parameters of the program. Ideally residents will learn to develop their own internal or intrinsic reasons for changing, yet programs still need to know if they are being ineffective or if additional resources may be needed. A general guideline may be "Is the resident moving in a positive direction? Is he or she engaging in treatment? Does the resident want to make a change? Is the resident making progress on his or her goals? What are the program deal breakers?

Understand why people use. Substances have multiple meanings and adaptive values to people. Help them identify alternative ways to get these needs met. For many people, residential placement is safe, nurturing, and comfortable; they may want to stay. It is common for residents to "sabotage" their discharge plans to allow for continued care. When this occurs, talk about it openly without judgment. Validate how important is it to feel safe and cared for. Talk about other ways to meet these vital needs and proactively work to allow for a transition where people are given increasingly more responsibility and independence so they can ease into the next environment.

Incorporate skills teaching that focuses on practical and useful skills. (See Chapter Six, The Key Skills.)

Develop ways to hold residents who use accountable. This can happen in many ways. Don't protect residents from the natural consequences of their use. When someone disrupts the program or therapeutic community, hold him or her accountable to the community, meaning the community is active in responding to the critical event. Needing to repair relationships within a community can be far more powerful than staff interventions.

Use voluntary restrictions (meaning the resident cannot leave the building) to help residents break the patterns of use and stay in the facility while he or she is experiencing the more acute withdrawal symptoms. Get the resident's input about how long or how broad the restriction may need to be. Have the resident complete a Substance Use Review Form when there is a use episode and have the resident review the homework with the treatment team or primary counselor. Have him or her work on agreements to build trust and integrity.

Cultivate an understanding that residents are responsible for their own safety and sobriety. Be clear and consistent that it is not the staff's responsibility to keep people safe and sober. We can help set up supports and teach skills but ultimately they decide what they are going to do. Be very clear that if someone is a serious health or safety threat to self or others, that staff will intervene and assume the locus of control. However, the doors are open, the setting is not a hospital and staff cannot prevent harmful behaviors.

Celebrate success and be very mindful to reinforce positive behaviors and not reinforce negative behaviors. We tend to get lost in the problems and may not spend enough energy rewarding the good things. Focusing on positives enhances the community and becomes self-rewarding. Pay attention, as it is easy to give a lot of energy to problematic behaviors and sometimes staff may need to remind each other about what behaviors they are reinforcing.

Manage your liability by reviewing and updating your policies and procedures. Don't claim to do more than is reasonable or realistic. You are at a greater risk of liability when you DO NOT do something you claim you are doing.

Ensure staff is trained in crisis intervention especially verbal de-escalation skills. Staff needs to be effective at calming individuals down. Empathy skills are vital.

Medical protocols need to be in place for substance use. Residents can be offered drug and alcohol testing (UAs) if they feel it will provide an external motivation. For example, someone may be worried about getting through the weekend, and may request a UA test be scheduled for Monday to help provide an incentive to help manage urges or high-risk situations. The client may request UAs for his or her own peace of mind, or for someone who may require testing such as probation or a family member. If the program culture promotes honesty, the "we are going to catch you" dynamic is nonexistent.

Program staff should have the skills to check vitals and have access to medical consultation. Poison control (1-800-222-1222) is a helpful resource and should be consulted whenever staff has questions about medication and/or medication interactions. Define the program's capacity to manage symptoms of withdrawal and when the resident may need more medical oversight.

Hire staff who embraces the harm reduction model. This often includes the following characteristics: high tolerance for ambiguity, open-mindedness, flexibility, not power-based, good boundaries, sense of humor, creative, patient, non-judgmental and most importantly a great deal of optimism and hope that people can recover.

Take the time to support the staff. Providing individualized treatment means the most common answer to any question is, "it depends". Very little is black and white or clear and simple. It is essential to have consistent consultation from supervisors and peers to talk through decisions and brainstorm clinical direction. Working as a team is critical for both solid clinical care and to support the staff to stay hopeful, compassionate, and effective.

This chapter has included information on mental health strategies, issues related to youth and young adults, and finally residential considerations. The next chapter focuses on broader system issues and the challenges of providing person-centered treatment systems that often require zero tolerance.

Chapter Nine

Systems Issues

It would be ideal if all clients under court oversight would embrace abstinence. Minnesota Alternatives encourages clients to take the necessary steps to resolve their legal problems, which often includes abstinence. However, many people decide to continue using substances while under commitment or on probation. Synthetic urine or supplements to "clean" urine are widely available. People are frequently trying to "beat" the system.

The treatment goals for "mandated" clients are the same as for voluntarily clients. Focus on engagement, encourage authenticity and honesty, and provide stage-specific interventions that include support, counseling, education, and accountability. If clients are determined to use, they will use. If they are engaged and open about their use, interventions can focus on ways to reduce risks to self and/or others and hopefully reduce future legal problems.

This chapter discusses ways to provide individualized, stage-specific treatment in systems that require abstinence. This chapter also list strategies that providers can use to help reduce risk and liability.

How to Integrate into Zero-Tolerance Systems Like Probation?

Serving clients who are mandated to abstain but have no intention to stop using, requires a combination of working to educate and challenge existing systems to embrace person-centered approaches and best practices, and remaining focused on the needs of the client.

Our client is not the courts or the probation officer. The primary obligation is to the person who has come for treatment. The goal of the program is to help people improve the quality of their lives, which often means progress not perfection. If a client is making positive movement in treatment, it should not cease because of a use episode or relapse.

Service coordination is essential, and working together with other providers is important for good client care. The community team may have different priorities, but all desire client success.

The program has had some success working with county authorities to change the language of civil commitment orders to read, "Will abstain from problematic use of mood-altering chemicals, or must comply with recommendations from the Minnesota Alternatives harm reduction program." This provides the "gray" needed for person-centered interventions. Working with correctional systems may seem more black and white, but probation officers all have their own "styles". Many are flexible and willing to support community tenure, even if clients are using, providing they can document progress and continued engagement.

Most professionals agree that clients have a better chance of gaining recovery through remaining in treatment, as opposed to going to jail or being locked up in an institution for months on end. The courts often need verification of enrollment, treatment progress, and program completion. Assuming the client is making progress and not jeopardizing public safety, information can be provided in a way that accurately reflects the client's process but leaves out the details. This is an effective way to permit the client to stay in treatment while still providing the necessary documentation.

An example of communication to the courts/probation:

- John Doe was admitted on this date and is making good progress on his goals.
- John Doe continues to participate in treatment and is making good progress on his goals.
- John Doe successfully completed treatment on this date.

Social workers and probation officers need progress reports but clients are assured that they are in control of what information gets shared. Programs cannot require clients under probation to sign a release of information in order for them to be served. If a client does not authorize open communication, this must be honored. Confidentiality is a right and failure to respect this is a serious violation.

On occasion, a client needs to be enrolled in an abstinence-based program per the requirements of the Department of Motor Vehicles. Under these circumstances, clients have a treatment plan that identifies a goal of abstinence while they are in treatment.

Mandatory AA

It is very common to see court orders requiring people to attend AA meetings. It can create resistance to mandate someone to a program or group he or she may disagree with. Can the system mandate self-help but let the client choose the approach?

Although the Supreme Court has yet to rule on this question, the current legal interpretation by the Ninth Circuit Court of Appeals is that mandating people by judges to attend 12-Step meetings is unconstitutional based on the Establishment Clause of the U.S. Constitution, commonly referred to as "the separation of church and state".[80]

AA Alternatives

Inrecovery.co is a website developed by a Twin Cities man that lists resources in this area for all types of recovery groups including AA alternatives.

Rational Recovery is a worldwide source of counseling, guidance, and direct instruction on self-recovery from addiction to alcohol and other drugs through planned, permanent abstinence. The group believes that individuals are on their own in staying sober, so there are no meetings or treatment centers as part of the approach. The website provides information about the method (Addictive Voice Recognition Technique® [AVRT®]), frequently asked questions, free information for those trying to stay sober (as well as their families), and information about subscription-based services.

Recovery, Inc. a self-help mental health program based on the work of its founder, the late Abraham A. Low, M.D., a neuropsychiatrist. Recovery, Inc. offers its members a free method to regain and maintain their mental health and is designed to work in conjunction with professional mental health services. The website provides information and background about the group, links to resources for group members and professionals, forum boards for discussions/support, and a directory of the over 700 group meetings in the U.S. and several other countries.

Secular Organizations for Sobriety (SOS) is an alternative recovery method for those alcoholics or drug addicts who are uncomfortable with the spiritual content of widely available 12-Step programs. SOS takes a secular approach to recovery and maintains that sobriety is a separate issue from religion or spirituality. The website provides more information about the organization, including the history, brochures about the group, as well as links to live meetings around the world.

SMART Recovery SMART (Self-Management and Recovery Training) Recovery® helps people recover from all types of addictive behaviors, including: alcoholism, drug abuse, substance abuse, drug addiction, alcohol abuse, gambling addiction, cocaine addiction, and addiction to other substances and activities. SMART Recovery® offers free face-to-face and online mutual help groups. The website provides extensive information about the SMART Recovery program, and contact information for over 750 face-to-face meetings worldwide (materials are available in eight languages), daily online meetings, online chat, and the message board (which are available 24/7).

---

[80] Egelko, B. (September 8, 2007) *San Francisco Chronicle,* "Appeals court says requirement to attend AA unconstitutional".

Women for Sobriety, Inc. is a non-profit organization dedicated to helping women overcome alcoholism and other addictions. Its "New Life" program is based upon a thirteen acceptance-statement program of positivity that encourages emotional and spiritual growth. The website provides additional information about the group, the thirteen statements of the program, and links to find groups in your area.

HAMS: Harm Reduction for Alcohol is a peer-led and free-of-charge support and informational group for anyone who wants to change their drinking habits for the better. The acronym HAMS stands for Harm Reduction, Abstinence, and Moderation Support. HAMS Harm Reduction strategies are defined in the 17 elements of HAMS. HAMS offers information and support via a chat room, an email group, and live meetings, as well as the articles on the web site.

LifeRing is a network of support groups for people who want to live free of alcohol and other addictive drugs. LifeRing encourage each participant to work out his or her own particular path and to use the group process as a workshop for that purpose. The main thing to remember is that the LifeRing process is strength-based; it works by positive reinforcement of qualities that you already have. The core unit of LifeRing is the recovery meeting. LifeRing works through positive social reinforcement. The meeting process empowers the Sober Self within each of us. Meeting locations and online support can be found at the web site: www.lifering.org

Managing Risk

There is no doubt it would be much easier to operate a program that practiced a "one size fits all" approach, using templates for treatment plans, requiring everyone to abstain, providing the same intensity and frequency to each and having one measure for success.

Individualized treatment is more complicated and remaining engaged with people who are actively using involves greater risk. It is important to do whatever you can to minimize risk and liability and then practice the skill of attached detachment. All we can do is our best and then let go. Don't get caught up in all that can go wrong and instead focus on all that is going well. The rewards of engagement, authenticity, and connection far outweigh the risks of personalized treatment.

Here are some strategies for risk management:

- **Remain mission driven.** This work can be overwhelming and confusing at times. The needs can far exceed the capacity of the program. Demand can be high – circumstances can trigger intense emotions. Whenever conflicting interests arise, anchor in the mission. This keeps the priorities clear and the program focused.

- **Focus on customer satisfaction.** Strive to create a treatment program that people come to because they find it helpful and a productive use of their time. Even if they don't "succeed" in the program, ensure they are treated with respect and communicate that the program has their best interests in mind. Some clients do not successfully complete the first or second time in the program, but many return because they were treated respectfully and welcomed during their previous experience.

- **Engage relevant others (family, natural supports) whenever possible.** If they perceive the program is trying it's best to help their loved one, they will be less likely to hold the program liable if there is a poor outcome. When permitted, engage them as part of the team to help with support and accountability. "Family" meetings are done with each individual family (instead of group education) to help ensure the unique needs of the family are addressed. For example, some family meetings may involve education, while others may address boundaries, self-care, and communication or limit setting.

- **Be clear about what you are doing.** Providers are at greater risk if they claim to be doing something they are not doing. Have a clearly defined scope of practice and do not claim to provide something that is not provided. For example, if a provider states they offer medical services and a medical complication goes undetected or unaddressed, the liability is greater than for the provider who does not include this in their scope of practice.

- **Document the important stuff and when possible use a team approach.** When it comes to risk management, reviewers will look for proper assessment and then planning and interventions that support the assessment. They will also look for the proper follow-up to ensure the risk factors are addressed. Ensure staff has adequate supervision and encourage them to seek consultation whenever needed. When possible, consult with case managers, therapists, and other service providers and document the nature of this consultation. Share the liability.

- **Incorporate legal language that calls for "will abstain from problematic use" instead of "will abstain from all use".** Offering individualized treatment often requires harm reduction interventions. Serving clients who are mandated by the court to abstain presents challenges as discussed at the beginning of this chapter. The program has received many referrals for clients on civil commitment because they are a good fit for harm reduction and flexible language like "will abstain from problematic use" allows for individualized and stage-specific interventions.

- **Have adequate staff/client ratios.** It is difficult to provide individualized treatment if clients are in large groups led by one staff. It is also difficult to intervene proactively if staff are extended and overworked. The program strives for a maximum group size of eight (for all process groups) and the program has enough staff on duty that someone is always available to meet individually when needed and/or in the event of a crisis.

- **Be skillful at de-escalating a crisis.** Staff is trained in crisis intervention (specifically the use of empathy skills). They know how to avoid power struggles, how to use effective verbal de-escalation skills and when to involve outside resources.

- **Staff is cross-trained in mental health.** Staff has training and experience in the field of mental health. They know how to assess and intervene with various mental illnesses including a basic understanding of psychotropic medications. They are able to effectively work with serious and persistent mental illnesses such as bi-polar, schizoaffective, schizophrenia, major depression, and personality disorders.

- **Informed Consent.** Clients read and sign an informed consent that explains that the program practices harm reduction and does not require goals of abstinence. Any use of drugs or alcohol is at their own risk.

- For example: I _____understand that Minnesota Alternatives practices a harm reduction approach and not everyone has abstinence as a recovery goal. I also understand that any continued use of drugs or alcohol is at my own risk and I will not hold Minnesota Alternatives responsible if problems occur as a result of my choice to use.

This chapter covered an array of strategies to provide an alternative treatment approach in systems of care that primarily require abstinence. The final chapter of this practice guide shares outcome information and concludes with clients' testimonials about their experiences.

Chapter Ten

Program Evaluation and Client Testimonial

Conventional programs generally measure clients' readiness for discharge by the number of days or sessions they have attended. They often require numerous packets to be completed, and most require that clients have a goal of abstinence.

Minnesota Alternatives uses other measures as indicators for success. As discussed earlier, clients graduate when they have accomplished their treatment goals and when they feel ready to manage their issues without the program support. Completion is not linked to the number of hours or days completed.

Goal completion is easy to measure, but a client's internal sense of readiness is less concrete. Generally, clients seem ready once they have put some other things in place that help support their recovery. This could be taking classes, a volunteer or paid job, self-help groups, joining a club, developing a new hobby, or developing more supports. Offering ongoing support for clients who have successfully completed the program helps them feel more secure about finishing as they know they can return weekly for continued support/accountability.

In addition to successful program completion, the program measures the following outcomes:

- Substance use
- Substance use-related harms/consequences
- Quality of life
- Stage of change
- Client satisfaction

It is important to note the demographic of the people served at Minnesota Alternatives. According to the Minnesota Reporting System, Drug and Alcohol Abuse Normative Evaluation System (DAANES), for 2011:

- The average age was 37 years old
- Men and women were equally represented
- 26% were disabled
- 62% had a mental illness

Clients are given brief surveys at admission and discharge to obtain the following information and copies of the surveys used can be found in the appendix.

Program Outcomes:

- The data below covers the period September 2009 to June 2012.

Successful Program Completion:

- 63% (115/184 total discharged) were discharged with staff approval. Of the 115 approved discharges, the following was reported.

Amount of Substance Use:

- Reduced use – 97%
- Increased use – 3%

Amount of Substance Use Related Harms/Consequences:

- Reduced consequences – 82%
- Increased areas – 8%
- Same level – 10%

Client Quality of Life (QOL):

- Increased QOL – 65%
- Same level – 30%
- Reduced QOL – 5%

Client Stage of Change:

- Maintained pre-contemplation stage – 2%
- Maintained contemplation stage – 2%
- Maintained action stage – 30%
- Maintained maintenance stage – 18%
- Movement forward along the stages – 45%
- Moved backward along the stages – 3%

Client Satisfaction:

- 4.73 on a scale of 1 to 5 with 5 being the highest score possible

12-Month Outcomes (October 201212) based on client survey:

Responses to the question "Please rate your quality of life":

- Very poor – my life is miserable – 10%
- Pretty rough, but some days are okay – 3%
- So-So – my life is okay, but it could be better – 13%
- Things are going pretty well for the most part – 57%
- My life is great; everything is going my way –16%

Responses to the question "Please describe the role of substance use in your life":

- I am not using at all. – 54%
- I am using in what I consider reasonable amounts and am not having any consequences from use. – 43%
- I am using more than I would like, and am having some consequences from use. – 0%
- My use is out of control and I am experiencing some problems as a result. – 3%

Response to the question "Have you been in the hospitalized for addiction or mental health issues since you were discharged?"

- No – 90%
- Yes – 10%

Response to the question "Have you had any other treatment since you were discharged?"

- No – 90%
- Yes – 10%

Another measure of satisfaction is daily client feedback received regarding how useful the client found the day's experience (see form titled Client Daily Feedback). This form provides daily information that can be used to make program changes and address client concerns as they occur.

There is a lot of work to be done to define what is effective and how to measure success, but there does appear to be one consistent finding:

If a program can engage and retain them, people will show positive change.

Client Testimonial

Here are some excerpts from clients who have received services at Minnesota Alternatives:

- As someone who has struggled with and confronted (with varying degrees of success) alcohol abuse for over 30 years, Minnesota Alternatives was a true breath of fresh air. My dependence on mood alteration through alcohol can be said to have resulted in a life of diminished expectations, i.e., "sins" of omission, more than of commission. So from the outside, my life did not resemble a picture of chaos that may afflict many who are chemically dependent. But I have caused myself a good deal of suffering, and had come to a dead-end place in my attempts to stop drinking alcohol in an abusive way.

  But I have always chaffed at the rigid goal of life-long abstinence. I believe that Minnesota Alternatives has given me useful tools for self-reflection and for accepting personal responsibility about important life choices. What I appreciate most was that my own ideas and intentions in this regard were given respect and credence. I have gained a lot of information and insight, and dare I say – wisdom – in my long struggle, which means that my treatment ought to be tailored to that process. And it was! It was co-developed with kindness, competence, professionalism, and good will on the part of the staff. There are no guarantees in this endeavor; my challenges are not over. But as a recent graduate of the program, my hopes are high and intentions solid, that I will continue this adventure of living without succumbing to the unhappy, unhealthy, and dangerous effects of alcohol abuse. – LL

- The program was very effective because of the ability to be honest and speak freely. I felt that when I spoke, people listened. The staff's willingness to help was outstanding, but personally the skills and the meditation were key for me. They gave me something to change my life that worked. I have been through other programs and felt good about myself, but never given skills to REALLY help me make changes. – GK

- The approach that Minnesota Alternatives uses is different in the fact that they use an individualized interpretation to bring a holistic perspective to all issues surrounding the client's addiction, relapses, and ongoing methods to endure a life-style that is conducive to recovery. The counselors' experience shows they are able to address mental health problems, medication management, family stressors, relationship conflicts, relapse triggers, negative re-occurring thought patterns and belief systems, and emotional instability. Minnesota Alternatives supports you in an "unconditionally" loving way, which is the only way you can support someone with addiction. You cannot will a 12-Step program on someone who isn't ready and Minnesota Alternatives staff is entirely devoted to people whoever or wherever they're at or how far they are willing to work. – JD

- I like the flexibility, the holistic approach, the small groups, and the supportive non-threatening nature of the program. The brain groups were very helpful, and the approach really made sense to me. – MG

- Unlike other chemical dependency treatment programs I've been in, Minnesota Alternatives seeks to empower each individual rather than babysit them or treat them as a number in the program. No other program challenged my intellect, taught me new skills, and brought out my emotions like Minnesota Alternatives did with the level of support that is offered there. The meditation exercises, daily readings, therapy, and skills discussions have helped me find myself again. – LH

- This program became the perfect fit for me. I trusted the staff enough to be able to get to the roots of my life-long problems. Without their help and understanding, I believe I would have never changed. I liked the meditation, the 1:1 time, the mindfulness walks, check-ins, and the chance to get to know people better. – DK

- Each person is looked at as an individual. We don't have to "fit your program". It is mine. – DP

- I most valued the committed 1:1 time, the openness and non-judgmental attitude, the harm reduction philosophy rather than rigid steps, and the incorporation of art. – KV

- The program was wonderful and addressed each and everything in my situation personally. I identified the reasons I chose to use and I was able to deal with situations from my past that needed to be brought up and dealt with. – BH

- I liked the individual program designed for each participant, the openness of communication, the attitude of each situation as unique, and as long as one has the desire to progress, the staff keeps "hanging in there". Slips are not kick-outs but are seen as opportunities for growth. – LB

- This is the first treatment program where I have felt safe. Other programs were very rigid and used a lot of confrontation. I became more anxious and would say what I thought staff wanted to hear to avoid getting in trouble. At Minnesota Alternatives, I can be honest. I feel respected, supported, and safe. – PP

Conclusion and Acknowledgements

Thank you for taking the time to read this practice guide.

As you know, treatment does not include any magic pills or silver bullets. All we can do is our best. We do our best, and then we let go. It is now time to "let go" of this book and "what happens, happens."

Thanks to the many people who offered their time to read, make suggestions and edit this text. These include: Charlie Bulman, Krissa Jackson, Ryan McKinney, Kenneth Anderson,

David Hanson, Kevin Turnquist, Bruce Field, Julie Rohovit, Tecla Karpen, Stanton Peele, Pamela Nelson, and Tom Horvath. Final editing was done by Mindy Beller.

Thanks to Rene' Trujillo for his amazing skills (cover design), help with selecting images, and for guiding the publication process.

Special thanks to my partner, Scott Sydor, for his patience and support, and for loving and accepting a very distracted (and sometimes irritable) girlfriend.

References

- Achor, S. (2010) *The Happiness Advantage. The Seven Principles of Positive Psychology That Fuel Success and Performance at Work.*

- *American Journal of Preventive Medicine* (1998) Volume 14, Issue 4 , "Relationship of Childhood Abuse and Household Dysfunction to Many of the Leading Causes of Death in Adults: The Adverse Childhood Experiences (ACE) Study".

- American Psychiatric Association (APA) (2000) *Diagnostic and Statistical Manual of Mental Disorders, 4th Edition*, Text Revision. Washington, DC: APA.

- Anderson, K. (2010) *How to Change Your Drinking* (Hamsnetwork.org).

- Barrash, J. Discovery of Self, The Continuum Center, Minneapolis MN.

- Baumeister, R., Tierney, J. (2011) *Willpower: Rediscovering the Greatest Human Strength.*

- Brauser, D., *Medscape Medical News, Psychiatry,* "Synthetic Cannabis May Pose an Even Greater Psychosis Risk".

- Brown L., Davis L., LaRocco, V., Strasburger, A. (2010) *American Journal of Psychiatric Rehabilitation* 13:3, 224-242, "Participant Perspectives on Mindfulness Meditation Training for Anxiety in Schizophrenia".

- Bundrant, M. (2011) *Natural News,* "Amino Acid Therapy for Depression, Anxiety, ADHD, Addiction and More".

- Cherry, K. *A Brief Overview of the Field of Positive Psychology.*

- Chen, K., & Kandel, D. (1995) *American Journal of Public Health*, 85 (1), 41-47, "The Natural History of Drug Use from Adolescence to the Mid-Thirties in a General Population Sample".

- Coppola M., Mondola R. (2012) *Toxicology Letters,* 211 (2): 144–149, "Synthetic Cathinones: Chemistry, Pharmacology, and Toxicology of a New Class of Designer Drugs of Abuse Marketed as "Bath Salts" or "Plant Food".

- Cozolino, L. (2010) *The Neuroscience of Psychotherapy: Healing the Social Brain* (2nd ed.) New York: Norton.

- Denning P., Little J. (2012) *Practicing Harm Reduction Psychotherapy*, 2nd Edition.

- Dispenza, J. (2007) *Evolve Your Brain: The Science of Changing Your Mind.*

- Dispenza, J. (2009) "Kidnapped by Technology" at www.joedispenza.com.

- Egelko, B. (September 8, 2007) *San Francisco Chronicle.* "Appeals Court Says Requirement to Attend AA Unconstitutional".

- *LiveScience.* "Fake Weed, Real Drug: K2 Causing Hallucinations in Teens". Retrieved November 24, 2010.

- Garland, Fredrickson, Kring , Johnson , Meyer, Penn (2010) Upward spirals of positive emotions counter downward spirals of negativity: Insights from the broaden-and-build theory and affective neuroscience on the treatment of emotion dysfunctions and deficits in psychopathology.

- Garcia, L. (2012) *Dallas Morning News,* "Stress Eats Holes in Your Brain".

- Gopnik, A. (2012) *The Wall Street Journal*, "What's Wrong With the Teenage Mind?"

- *Global Commission on Drug Policy Report* (2011) "The War on Drugs and HIV/AIDS: How the Criminalization of Drug Use Fuels the Global Pandemic".

- Governor's Commission on Sexual and Domestic Violence (2006), Commonwealth of MA

- Hanson, R., Mendius R. (2009) *The Practical Neuroscience of Buddha's Brain.*

- Wiley-Interscience, "Healing Addiction: An Integrated Pharmacopsychosocial Approach to Treatment", 2007, p. 122.

- Hunt, N. (2010) "A Review of the Evidence-Base for Harm Reduction Approaches to Drug Use". Available at www.ihra.net

- Harm Reduction Coalition, "Principles of Harm Reduction", available at http://harmreduction.org/.

- Hesse, C., Floyd, K., (2011) *Journal Personality and Individual Differences*, 18(3):453-470, "Affection Mediates the Impact of Alexithymia on Relationships" .

- SAMSHA Toolkit, "Illness Management and Recovery (IMR)"

- Jellinekk, E. (1960). "The Disease Concept of Alcoholism". New Haven, CT: Hillhouse.

- Kelly, B. (2011) Deptartment of Psychological Brain Science, Dartmouth College. Workshop on Bad Habit Prevention.

- Larson J.M., Ph.D. (1992) *Seven Weeks to Sobriety*. New York: Fawcett Columbine.

- Lewis, M. (2011) *Memoirs of an Addicted Brain*.

- Louwagie, P (2011) *Star Tribune*, "Bath Salts Hit U.S. 'Like a Freight Train'".

- Maté, G. (2010) "In the Realm of Hungry Ghosts".

- McGonigal, K. (2011) "The Science of Willpower: How Mindfulness Makes the Brain Immune to Temptation".

- Mikuriya, T.H. (2004) Journal of Cannabis Therapeutics. Vol. 4(1), "Cannabis as a Substitute for Alcohol: A Harm-Reduction Approach".

- Morgan, et al. (2002) *Nature Neuroscience* 5, 169 – 174, "Social Dominance in Monkeys: Dopamine D2 Receptors and Cocaine Self-Administration"

- Mueser, Noodsy, Drake, Fox (2003) *Integrated Treatment for Dual Disorders: A Guide to Effective Practice*

- Miller, W. R., Zweben, A., DiClemente, C. C., & Rychtarik, R. G. (1992) *Motivational Enhancement Therapy Manual.*

- *New South Wales Public Health Bulletin*, Mar-Apr;21(3-4):69-73 (2010). "Is Harm Reduction Effective?"

- *Newsweek Magazine* (2012) July 2012 Cover Story: "iCrazy: Panic. Depression. Psychosis. How Connection Addiction is Rewiring our Brains".

- National Institute of Alcoholism and Alcohol Abuse (2012) "Alcoholism Isn't What It Used To Be".

- National Institute of Alcoholism and Alcohol Abuse (2006) "National Epidemiologic Survey on Alcohol and Related Conditions (NESARC) #70".

- National Institute of Drug Abuse (2009) *Principles of Effective Treatment: A Research-Based Guide (2nd edition) Pharmacotherapies.*

- National Institute of Drug Abuse (2009) *Principles of Effective Treatment: A Research Based Guide (2nd edition).*

- National Institute of Drug Abuse (2009) *Drugs, Brains, and Behavior: The Science of Addiction.*

- Olson, J. (2011) *Star Tribune*, "If Troubled Kids Aren't Bipolar, Then What is Troubling Them?"

- Plummer, J. (2005) Unpublished Manuscript, "Substance abuse treatment capacity: Childhood physical and sexual abuse and neglect has a staggering impact on the prevalence of substance abuse in adulthood: current treatment capacity is inadequate to meet the need."

- Prochaska, J. O., DiClemente, C. C. (2005) "The Transtheoretical Approach". In: Norcross, JC; Goldfried, MR. (eds.) *Handbook of Psychotherapy Integration. 2nd ed.* New York: Oxford University Press.

- Peterson, C. (2006) *A Primer in Positive Psychology*, New York, NY: Oxford University Press.

- Reiman, A, (2009) *Harm Reduction Journal* 6(35), "Cannabis as a Substitute for Alcohol and Other Drugs".

- Robin, L. N., Helzer, J. E., Hesselbrock, M., Wish, E. (1980). *Yearbook of Substance Use and Abuse.* New York: Human Science Press, "Vietnam Veterans Three Years After Vietnam: How Our Study Changed Our View of Heroin".

- SAMHSA Press Release (2011) "SAMHSA Announces a Working Definition of "Recovery" from Mental Disorders and Substance Use Disorders".

- SAMHSA Press Release (2010) "Office of Applied Studies. The N-SSATS Report. Clinical or Therapeutic Approaches Used by Substance Abuse Treatment Facilities". Rockville, MD: US Dept. of Health and Human Services.

- SAMHSA Treatment Improvement Protocol #35, "Enhancing Motivation for Change in Substance Abuse Treatment".

- SAMHSA Treatment Improvement Protocol #42, "Substance Abuse Treatment for Persons with Co-Occurring Disorders".

- *Science Daily* (July 18, 2011) "New Discoveries by Researchers at the University of Wisconsin-Milwaukee (UWM) Offer Potential for Development of a First-Ever Pharmacological Treatment for Cocaine Addiction".

- Seligman, M. E. P. (2002). Authentic Happiness: Using the New Positive Psychology to Realize Your Potential for Lasting Fulfillment.

- Shore, R. (1997) Citing Data from Rethinking the Brain: New Insights into Early Development.

- Siegel, D. J. (2010) *Mindsight: The New Science of Personal Transformation*. New York: Bantam Books.

- Sigillata, T. (2010) What's the buzz? Synthetic marijuana, K2, Spice, JWH-018: Scienceblogs.com. Retrieved November 24, 2010.

- Szalavitz, M. (2010) *Time Magazine*, "Does Teen Drug Rehab Cure Addiction or Create It?"

- Tervalon, M.,& Murray-Garcia, J. (1998) *Journal of Health Care for the Poor and Underserved*, "Cultural Humility Versus Cultural Competence: A Critical Distinction in Defining Physician Training Outcomes in Multicultural Education".

- Tevlin, J. (2012) *Star Tribune*, March 17, "Forgiveness, Hope Wins Out Over Crime in Juvenile Court"s.

- Turnquist, K – www.kevinturnquist.org – "New Models of the Mind, The Neurobiology of Loneliness, The Use of Benzodiazepines".

- Willenbring, M – www.alltyr.com – Substance Matters - Alltyr Blog "Benzos for Recovering People?, Potential New Treatment for Cocaine Addiction?"

Appendix of Handouts

- Understanding Motives or Reasons for Substance Use
- Understanding Negative Consequences of Substance Use
- Evaluating Pros and Cons of Use
- Plan for Managing High-Risk Situations
- Client Review For Substance Use
- Self-Monitoring Log
- Personal Agreement
- Admission Outcome Survey
- Discharge Outcome Survey
- 12-Month Post-Discharge Outcome Survey
- Client Daily Feedback
- Sample Harm Reduction Individual Treatment Plan
- The Key Skills
- Skills Mastery Grid

Understanding Motives or Reasons for Substance Use

Name _____ Date _____

My primary substance is _____

Check all the reasons why you use and also circle the top 3 reasons:

____ To relieve physical pain   ____ To be social/party with friends
____ To ease anxiety   ____ To cope with depression
____ To deal with difficult emotions   ____ To connect more with God/Spirit
____ To sleep better   ____ It has become a ritual/habit
____ To numb out   ____ To become more introspective
____ To get a thrill or rush   ____ To deal with boredom
____ For sexual release/pleasure   ____ To cope with past traumatic events
____ To experience euphoria   ____ To enhance music or other art forms
____ To fit in with friends   ____ To cope with _____
____ To relax and feel more calm   ____ Other reasons: _____
____ To unwind after a hard day

Please list and explain the top 3 reasons for use:

1. _____
   _____

2. _____
   _____

3. _____
   _____

Take a moment and examine each of the 3 reasons you listed.

Can you come up with any alternative ways to fill these needs or wants? Yes No
If yes, what are some alternatives?

Do you need help resolving some issues that contribute to your use? Yes No

If yes, what issues need to be resolved?

Reviewed by _____ Date _____

Understanding Negative Consequences of Substance Use

Name _____ Date _____

Please check any consequences you have experienced from your substance use:

____ Health issues
____ Legal Issues
____ Relationship problems
____ Money issues
____ Housing issues
____ Compromising my values
____ Breaking the law
____ Dishonesty
____ Putting my safety/life in danger
____ At risk of going to jail/prison
____ At risk of losing my child or children
____ Losing people I care about
____ Hospitalization
____ Mental health symptoms getting worse
____ Conflicts with others
____ I let others down
____ I get taken advantage of
____ Job problems
____ Mood problems
____ Others _____

I completed research of the harmful effects of primary substance on this date: _____
Summary of key findings:

Reviewed by _____ Date _____

Evaluating Pros and Cons of Use

Name _____   Date_____

Please list the pros and cons of continued use of your primary substance. Do as many as you need and it may need to be repeated at different times. If struggling with multiple substances, complete one for each.

Pros or advantages of continued use:	Cons or consequences of continued use:

I plan to:
_____ Cut down or change my use pattern
Thoughts:

_____ Quit and remain abstinent
Thoughts:

_____ Uncertain
Thoughts:

Reviewed by _____   Date _____

Plan for Managing High-Risk Situations

Name _____   Date _____

Identify your top three high-risk situations and come up with a plan for how you will manage them. Include key skills you plan to use, actions you will take, people you will call, etc. Be as detailed as possible.

1. Situation:

   _____

   _____

   Plan, including skills I would use:

   _____

   _____

2. Situation:

   _____

   _____

   Plan, including skills I would use:

   _____

   _____

3. Situation:

   _____

   _____

   Plan, including skills I would use:

   _____

   _____

Each situation needs to be role played or discussed with a staff or peer. Please list the date you role played or discussed each high-risk situation:

Reviewed by _____   Date _____

Client Review for Substance Use

Please complete the following form as soon as possible after your use episode. The purpose is to better understand your choice to use and to identify possible changes to your treatment plan.

Name _____ Date Reviewed _____

1. What triggered your urge to use?

   a. Thoughts:
   b. Feelings:
   c. Events:

2. Before your use did you try to use any skills or seek support?   Yes/No

If yes, circle the skills you tried: Self Care, Calming, Experiencing Emotions, Building Positive Experiences, Cultivating Hope and Gratitude, Reframing, Practicing Acceptance, Understanding Impermanence, Focusing on Effectiveness, Developing Meaningful Activity

- Others:_____

- Were the skills helpful? _____

- Did you try to reach out to anyone? If so, who and what happened?_____

If no, why not?_____

3. What benefits did you experience from the use?

4. What consequences did you experience from the use?

5. Are you having any symptoms of withdrawal? If so, what are you experiencing?

6. Are you satisfied with the progress you are making in your recovery? Yes/No
   If no, what needs to change?

7. Does your treatment plan need to be changed? If yes, what suggestions do you have?

8. Anything else you would like to discuss?

Self-Monitoring Log

Name _____

Date and Time:	Type and amount used:	Benefits of Use:	Consequences of Use:	Reflections:

Personal Agreement

Date:_____

Name:_____

I agree to the following:

The purpose of this agreement is to provide accountability and build integrity as I work to make new choices and change behaviors.

Each written agreement should include a handshake and solid eye-to-eye contact.

Signature _____

Agreeing other party _____

Admission Outcome Survey

Please complete at **admission** to the program.

Client Name_____ Date Completed_____

Please list the amount and types of drugs and/or alcohol you are **currently** using. If you were in a secure facility or hospital right before coming to treatment, please list the amounts used **before you were locked up**.

Please check any type of harm that is occurring in your life related to your substance use:

____ Health issues
____ Legal issues
____ Relationship problems
____ Money issues
____ Housing issues
____ Compromising my values
____ Breaking the law
____ Dishonesty
____ Putting my safety/life in danger
____ At risk of going to jail/prison
____ At risk of losing my child or children
____ Losing people I care about
____ Hospitalization
____ Mental health symptoms getting worse
____ Conflicts with others
____ I let others down
____ I get taken advantage of
____ Job problems
____ Mood problems
____ Others _____

Please rate your **quality of life** by circling the number that best matches how you feel **overall** about your life.

1 – Very poor – my life is miserable
2 – Pretty rough, but some days are okay
3 – So-So – my life is okay, but it could be better
4 – Things are going pretty well for the most part
5 – My life is great, everything is going my way

Please list your current **stage of change**: (If you are not sure ask staff)

____ Precontemplation – "I do not have a problem."
____ Contemplation – "I may have a problem, but I am not sure."
____ Action – "I definitely have a problem and I am doing something about it."
____ Maintenance – "I have been doing pretty well and I just need to keep maintaining."

Discharge Outcome Survey

Please complete at **discharge from** the program.

Client Name_____ Date Completed_____

Please list the amount and types of drugs and/or alcohol you are currently using.

Please check any type of harm that is occurring in your life related to your substance use:
____ Health issues
____ Legal Issues
____ Relationship problems
____ Money issues
____ Housing issues
____ Compromising my values
____ Breaking the law
____ Dishonesty
____ Putting my safety/life in danger
____ At risk of going to jail/prison
____ At risk of losing my child or children
____ Losing people I care about
____ Hospitalization
____ Mental health symptoms getting worse
____ Conflicts with others
____ I let others down
____ I get taken advantage of
____ Job problems
____ Mood problems
____ Others _____

Please rate your **quality of life** by circling the number that best matches how you feel **overall** about your life.

1 – Very poor – my life is miserable

2 – Pretty rough, but some days are okay

3 – So-So – my life is okay, but it could be better

4 – Things are going pretty well for the most part

5 – My life is great, everything is going my way

Discharge Outcome Survey – page 2

Please list your current **stage of change**: (If you are not sure ask staff)
____ Precontemplation – "I do not have a problem."
____ Contemplation – "I may have a problem, but I am not sure."
____ Action – "I definitely have a problem and I am doing something about it."
____ Maintenance – "I have been doing pretty well and I just need to keep maintaining."

Please rate your overall **level of satisfaction** with the program:

1 – Very poor

2 – Dissatisfied for the most part

3 – So-So – some was good, and some not so good

4 – Overall satisfied

5 – Very satisfied

Please list what you liked about the program:

Please list how you think the program can improve:

Client Signature _____

12-Month Post-Discharge Outcome Survey

Client Name_____ Date Completed_____

- Please rate your quality of life by circling the number that best matches how you feel overall about your life.

    1 – Very poor – my life is miserable
    2 – Pretty rough, but some days are okay
    3 – So-So – my life is okay, but it could be better
    4 – Things are going pretty well for the most part
    5 – My life is great, everything is going my way

- Please describe the role of substance use in your life:

    ____ I am not using at all.
    ____ I am using in what I consider reasonable amounts and am not having any consequences from use.
    ____ I am using more than I would like to, and am having some minor consequences from use.
    ____ My use is out-of-control and I am experiencing some problems as a result.

- Have you been in the hospital since you were discharged?
  If yes, where and for what reason?

- Have you had any other treatment since you were discharged?

- Anything else you would like to share?

Client Daily Feedback

Today's Date _____

Please rate today's treatment session: Circle one

Very useful   Useful enough   Not useful   A waste of my time
      4   3   2   1

Comments:

Client Daily Feedback

Today's Date _____

Please rate today's treatment session: Circle one

Very useful   Useful enough   Not useful   A waste of my time
      4   3   2   1

Comments:

Sample Harm Reduction Individual Treatment Plan

Recovery Vision: I feel healthy upon waking and I am on good terms with my family. I've developed a sober, supportive network of friends that I can have fun with.

Dimensions:	Problem:	Goals:	Methods/Objectives to Achieve the Goal :	Due and Completion Dates:
1) Acute Intoxication/ Withdrawal Potential:	Has history of polysubstance dependence – primary concern is heroin.	To abstain from all use of opiates and any problematic use of cannabis or alcohol.	Engage in treatment and attend at least one time per week.	1/wk
2) Biomedical Conditions:	No health issues.	Maintain good health.	Do yoga at least one time per week. Participate in alternative therapies and try a session of Reiki.	1/wk By____
3) Emotional/ Behavioral/ Cognitive Conditions:	Experiences depression and anxiety.	Manage mental health and feel less anxious and depressed. Share thoughts and feelings, and feel more confident.	Use breathing and mindfulness daily. Meditate at least 20 minutes 5 times per week. Practice talking more loudly to build confidence.	Daily 5/wk Daily
4) Treatment Acceptance/ Resistance:	Family pressure to attend but is open to the process.	Stay open and share any concerns as they arise.	Complete and review treatment worksheets that explore motives for use and pros and cons of use.	By____
5) Relapse/ Continued Use/ Continued Problem Potential:	Has history of polysubstance dependence – primary concern is heroin. Recent episode of	To reduce use and abstain from all problematic use. Stay off opiates.	Complete and review worksheet that identifies negative consequences. Complete and review my plan to manage high risk situations.	By____ By____

	serious overdose.		Abstain from any use of heroin and other opiates.	Daily
			If choosing to drink, limit use to no more than 4 drinks one time per week and do not drink and drive.	Weekly
			Do not purchase marijuana and smoke only when with others max 1 time per week.	Daily
6) Recovery Environment Family/Natural Supports Involvement:	Some family tension due to drug and alcohol use. A lot of social situations that involve drug and alcohol use. Unemployed.	Improved family relation-ships and social time with friends that does not involve heavy drug use. Doing well in school and working part-time.	Continue to do well in college and maintain at least a 3.2 GPA.	By ____
			Get together with friends to play music a couple times per week.	1/wk
			Avoid friends I used to use with.	Daily
			Continue to improve relationship with parents as evidenced by better communication and more positive experiences together.	By ____
			Find a job.	ASAP

The Key Skills

- **Practicing Basic Self Care** – Eat, sleep, exercise, drink water, and go outside to be with nature. I am less vulnerable if I am rested and fed. Quit polluting my brain and my body.

- **Calming Self through Breathing and Mindfulness** – Slow down and breathe deeply. Do not act. Allow the impulse to pass. Be mindful by noticing what is around me and try to be present in the moment.

- **Creating an Optimal Environment** – Everyone needs safety, connection with others, privacy, and order. Pay attention to my environment and who I surround myself with. Understand boundaries.

- **Experiencing Emotions** – Allow myself to experience difficult emotions by naming them, noticing how they feel in my body, stepping away from the story, and waiting for the sensations in my body to fade away. Ride the wave of the emotion.

- **Building Positive Experiences** – Create new neural networks based on positive memory, positive experiences, and positive emotions. Use imagery/visualization. Laughter neutralizes the negative effects of stress.

- **Cultivating Hope and Gratitude** – Choose to be hopeful, take time to notice all I am doing well and focus on my strengths and blessings. Learn to let go and practice forgiveness if I am holding onto resentments/anger.

- **Reframing** – Use my executive brain functions to decide the meaning I want to attach to circumstances. Learn to watch my thoughts and interrupt negative thought patterns. Meditation helps me train my mind and learn to focus.

- **Practicing Acceptance** – Refusing to accept situations I am unable to change only adds to my suffering. It is what it is.

- **Understanding Impermanence** – Remind myself that nothing is constant and these hard times will pass. Things will get better.

- **Practicing Attached Detachment** – Do my very best in life and then let go of the outcomes. Keep things in perspective.

- **Focusing on Effectiveness** – Pay attention to the goal I desire, and if needed, put aside pride or stubbornness and do what works. Be effective.

- **Demonstrating Understanding** – People are more likely to listen to me if I first demonstrate that I hear them.

- **Developing Meaningful Activity** – Find something to do that gives my life meaning and purpose.

Skills Mastery Grid

Name _____

Self-rate your level of mastery with each skill using any type of scale you prefer.
One option is +, +/-, or -.

Skill Name:	Date:	Date:	Date:	Date:	Date:	Date:	Date:	Date:
Practicing Basic Self Care								
Calming Self through Breathe/Mindfulness								
Creating an Optimal Environment								
Experiencing Emotions								
Building Positive Experiences								
Cultivating Hope and Gratitude								
Reframing								
Practicing Acceptance								
Understanding Impermanence								
Practicing Attached Detachment								
Focusing on Effectiveness								
Demonstrating Understanding								
Developing Meaningful Activity								
Add Personally Important or Other Essential Skills:								

Made in the USA
Middletown, DE
14 February 2017